BEING YOUR BEST!

If It Weren't For Your Ego

N.J. Mayfield

ISBN 0-7414-2687-0

Published by:

INFINITY
PUBLISHING.COM

1094 New DeHaven Street, Suite 100
West Conshohocken, PA 19428-2713
Info@buybooksontheweb.com
www.buybooksontheweb.com
Toll-free (877) BUY BOOK
Local Phone (610) 941-9999
Fax (610) 941-9959

Printed in the United States of America

Printed on Recycled Paper

Published October 2005

Table of Contents

Dedication

This book is dedicated to all of the Ego-Defensive people who have passed through my life. They made this book both possible and imperative.

Acknowledgments

I would like to express my deepest gratitude to the people who read this book and suggested improvements. They are (in alphabetical order):

Andrew Hall

Margaret Hart

Erskine Ramsay Kelly

Jim Lippert

Morris Massey, Ph.D.

Captain Arlie J. Nixon

Mary Ostrand

Special thanks to Dr. James M. Thomas, Jr. for encouraging me to write this and to Margaret Hart who provided invaluable help with the title.

Also, very special thanks to the members of our small writers' critique group for their continued help and support:

James William Brand

Betty Ellen Cole, Ph.D.

William J. Nelson, Ph.D.

You didn't let me get away with anything.

Introduction:

Why Should You Read This Book?

This book distills more than one hundred hours of psychotherapy into a simple, but powerful, program that can be implemented in a single day!

Out of all those therapy sessions, only one brief moment made a difference in my life. But the insight that then occurred immediately reversed what had been downward spirals of hope and of self-esteem and of the future.

My only regret is that the program presented in this book was not available to me when I was a teenager. Because of that, fifteen years of my life were essentially wasted. That is not to say that my life is a dismal failure. Many would say that it has been unusually successful. But, it became that way only after I replaced the pecking-order *Ego-Defensive* view of the world and myself with the freedom available through an *Ego-Neutral* perspective.

By following the guidelines in this book, *you can* make your life better. Today!

The method is really very simple, so don't make it difficult. Just keep in mind that *you* must *actually try* this program for yourself before you are in a position to judge whether or not it can be helpful for you.

Granted, there is more than one potential source of unhappiness.

- Situational factors making your current existence unpleasant (e.g., not enough money, a dead-end job, surrounded by disagreeable people).

- Brain and body chemistry conditions. For example, your metabolism may not adequately support a feeling of well-being. This can be observed in some forms of depression. Or, your brain chemistry may impair your perception and memory so that it is difficult for you to pursue and attain your goals. This happens, for example, in some types of schizophrenia or when you are sleep-deprived. Hormones from physical or mental stress can also affect the brain.

- The belief that others don't think well (or well enough) of you. *This issue is the focus of this book.*

A person can be unhappy from just one of the above conditions. Frequently, however, distress arises from the simultaneous impact of two or three factors.

In order to deal with unhappiness effectively, it is helpful to *first* address this issue: what you think others think of you. This mindset I have labeled ***Ego-Defensive***. The solution is to become ***Ego-Neutral***, as described in this book.

Why is it important to become Ego-Neutral first?

- It is the one approach over which *you* have complete control. You can do it simply by deciding to do it and by following the guidelines presented in this book. You can do it *today*!

- Once you have become Ego-Neutral, the intensity of your unhappiness should be noticeably reduced if not eliminated. When you are Ego-Neutral, you can then evaluate any remaining unhappiness and decide if it is something that you still want to address.

- Your coping skills should improve. Once you become Ego-Neutral, the way in which you view situational factors may change.

✓ You may realize that things weren't so bad after all.

✓ You may discover that your own Ego-Defensive behavior created or contributed to bad situations.

✓ You may discover a more effective way of addressing unpleasant conditions.

- Finally, you are in a position to identify the source of residual unhappiness as a brain-chemistry matter. You have done this by successfully eliminating the other two factors first. What remains can be attributed to physical factors. Dealing with the impact of body upon mind is not the focus of this book. I will simply say that mental and emotional composure may be addressed through more adequate sleep, increased exposure to full-spectrum light, improved diet, and use of nutritional supplements or prescription drugs.

Pills may not remove discomfort originating from an Ego-Defensive condition. For example, when you try a medication and remain unhappy, the medication might be one that would have improved your emotional state had you been Ego-Neutral. However, in your Ego-Defensive frame of mind, the positive effects from the medication may be distorted by the overwhelming unhappiness arising from your unresolved ego-related issues. So you go on to the next pill and the next pill and the pill after that, and none of them seem to work. You will never return to the first pill, since you have already concluded that it did not work. Had you been Ego-Neutral *before* or *while* modifying your brain chemistry, you would have been able to identify strictly brain-chemistry issues with greater accuracy.

Hopefully, you now understand why it is important to address all sources of unhappiness with methods specifically appropriate to each category. Also, hopefully, you now understand why it is useful to become Ego-Neutral first. If you are already on medication, continue taking it. However, keep in mind that becoming Ego-Neutral can still improve your life, by making self-esteem a non-issue.

In contrast to today's pill-dependent culture, this book provides you with an entirely *self-administered, non-chemical* program to transform yourself. Your life can be better, starting today!

QUIZ

With which of these statements do you agree?

1. I envy or resent successful people.

2. When I walk into a room, I feel like everyone is looking at me.

3. If I had a more glamorous job, I would be happy.

4. If I were smarter (prettier, richer, funnier – pick one or more), people would admire me and then I would be happy.

5. I don't care what people think about me, as long as they do what I say.

6. It is essential for others (especially popular, important or powerful people that I look up to) to like and/or admire me.

7. If I had an important, popular, rich, or powerful boyfriend/girlfriend, then everyone would think that I was important, popular, rich or powerful and then I would be happy.

8. If I do things by myself, people will think there is something wrong with me because no one else is doing these things with me.

9. If I were important, I would be happy.

10. I need to always have people around so others will think I am likable. If I'm alone, everyone will know that no one likes me.

11. If I make people afraid of me, then I'll be important (powerful, respected).

12. If I always point out faults in others, people will think I am observant and intelligent.

13. If I always point out weaknesses in the ideas of others, people will think I am observant and intelligent.

14. I'm extremely embarrassed when someone points out that I am wrong.

15. If I control everyone around me, then no one can control me and I can have everything I want with no bad consequences for me. That will make me happy.

16. I want to be rich and famous so I can do *anything* I want.

17. When I walk into a room, I feel like everyone is laughing at me.

18. Male heterosexuals: Whenever I score with some chick, afterward, I enjoy telling people what a slut she is.

19. Female heterosexuals: When some guy, who isn't what I'm looking for in a man, shows interest in me, I enjoy laughing about him with my friends.

20. I enjoy shocking people.

21. When I am admired, I am happy.

22. I enjoy offending people.

23. I enjoy it when I'm the center of attention.

24. After I perform a good deed, I go around telling everyone what I did.

25. When I give someone a gift, and they are not as delighted as I anticipated, I take it as a personal insult.

Agreement with any of these statements indicates that you are entangled in the control of a personal-power continuum called the *pecking order*. It also means that one or more of the following statements describes your perception of your position in the pecking order and your strategies for improving your position.

- You see your own position as lower in the social order than you desire.

- You feel the need to maintain or improve your position in the social order by forcing others into a position below yours.

- You seek to improve your social position by associating with social superiors as though they were equals.

- You are more concerned about the opinion others have of you than you are about seeking your own satisfactions.

- You can never find a long-term partner who is perfect enough to compensate for all of the faults you see in yourself.

- You are imprisoned in the pecking order.

Now read Section 1.

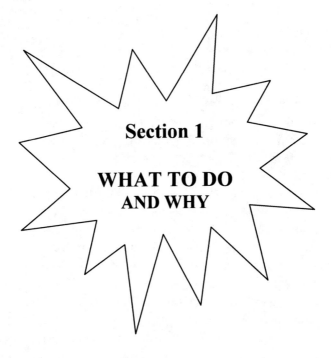

Section 1

WHAT TO DO
AND WHY

Are You a Believer
or an Investigator?

Frequently, people hold such deeply ingrained convictions that they are not even aware that these **are** beliefs. Instead, they view these convictions as being facts, which are set in concrete. Therefore, the beliefs are never questioned. Belief is a *conviction* of the truth of a concept, observation or conclusion. It is *not* open to speculation or testing.

In subsequent chapters, you are going to identify and examine some of those self-defeating beliefs that you have come to feel are facts and which are preventing you from seeing what may really be the truth.

An investigator pursues knowledge through observation, use of a working hypothesis, and experimentation. The working hypothesis is a temporary speculation, which is used to explain some known facts **and** to predict the occurrence of previously unobserved events.

For example, I am now relating an observation: By following the guidelines found in this section of the book, my life became substantially better. If you now *tentatively* conclude that by following the same guidelines, your life also might become better, **you have just developed a working hypothesis.** You *test* this working hypothesis by following those guidelines and observing whether or not your life becomes better. If your life does become better, the working hypothesis has been confirmed. If your life does not become better after the test, you discard that hypothesis and either return to your previous belief or develop a new working hypothesis.

In order to make your life better, you are going to have to *try* something that you are not doing now. It is not enough to read this book and decide, "This is too simple. It can't work for me." If you refuse to try, you have allowed your inflexible beliefs to keep you **imprisoned**. In this case, the belief is that simple changes cannot make an important difference in your life. Once you have actually executed the simple changes, you **then** can decide with certainty whether or not it works for you.

You will naturally hesitate to abandon your cherished beliefs. After all, they have guided nearly every waking moment of your recent life. Remember! You can always revert to the inadequate and harmful strategies that made you unhappy enough to begin reading this book in the first place. You will not need to permanently abandon your old mindset until you have a firm grasp of a more productive way to think and feel about the world and about yourself.

Basics for Attaining a Better Life

Some of these things may sound like they are coming from a preaching parent. I know it's a stretch, but *parents aren't wrong all of the time*. However, they frequently fail to explain the mindset that is needed to accompany certain actions. Also, they may not explain **why** these strategies work. By reading this book, you will understand why these strategies work and why it is to your benefit to behave in this way. Recognizing the Ego-Neutral mental state and applying it to your life, PLUS incorporating the following behaviors and activities into your daily activities, *can* turn things around for you.

If you need to immediately feel good about yourself, this program will not do it. *This is not about building self-esteem. This is about making self-esteem a non-issue.* The guidelines in this chapter **will improve** your life. Remember that I am not promising an ecstatic existence of perpetual self-aggrandizement. However, if you are not already Ego-Neutral, I am revealing steps to an easily attainable and sustainable better life than the one you have now.

- **Search for the complete truth in a situation.** Gather as many facts as possible before speaking. If you have a paranoid, Ego-Defensive mindset, put it on hold and ask yourself, what if this event is something else?

  ✓ Ask others what their impression of the situation is and why they believe that. *This is not the same thing as having others tell you how to think and feel.* This is information gathering by assuming different points of view. In the end, you will be drawing your *own* conclusions.

  ✓ Also, look to yourself for information. For example, if you find yourself habitually craving a cigarette or alcohol, ask, "What is it I am trying not to deal

8

with?" Then ask yourself, "Will a cigarette or alcohol make that problem disappear?" The answer is probably, "No." The best that the cigarette or alcohol can do is temporarily postpone a dreaded confrontation. Get it over with! Attack the REAL problem and stop draining away your life with destructive tools of procrastination.

- **Competing responses.** These are behaviors that cannot happen at the same time. Use a competing response when a situation makes you feel anxious. Also, competing responses are used to end addictive behaviors. When you feel uncomfortable with a situation, get busy! If you find yourself feeling uncomfortable in a group, find something constructive to do, which is relevant to the situation. For example, if the event requires tickets at the door and this is an event where you might end up standing alone talking to no one, see if you can help take the tickets. In a church social function, food is frequently involved. See if you can help with the serving or washing dishes. If you are in a computer group, try to learn what others are discovering or learning by listening and asking questions. If you crave a cigarette, suck on a straw instead of smoking. *When you are intensely focused on performing a task or gaining information, you cannot at the same time engage in Ego-Defensive perceptions, emotions and addictive behaviors.*

- The discussion in the next chapter will enable you to identify the genuine outward-focused, non-self-conscious Ego-Neutral emotional and perceptual set that you must invoke in all of your interactions in life. Review that chapter every single day until recognizing that Ego-Neutrality becomes second nature for you.

- Consistently follow these guidelines for behavior:
  - ✓ **ALWAYS** Be Honest With Yourself and strive to be honest with others.

- ✓ Be Reliable.

- ✓ Be Polite.

- ✓ Be Clean and Neat in Appearance.

- ✓ Don't be a show-off.

- ✓ Embark on self-improvement goals that require skill, rather than the approval of others, in order for you to succeed. A constructive, goal-oriented existence is *essential* for a satisfying life.

- ✓ Expand your opportunities for sharing activities with a wider variety of people. This can be combined with the previous step.

- Daily, remind yourself that it is **impossible** for you to *make* people like and respect you. However, you *can* keep the door open for people to enter your life and for you to be invited by others into their lives. You can accomplish this by avoiding behaviors that drive others away. Adhere to the above guidelines and transform your Ego-Defensive issues into an Ego-Neutral strategy of interfacing with the world.

How Does Ego-Neutral Feel?

You have been in an Ego-Neutral frame of mind numerous times before, **but without recognizing its importance**. Even now, you may be in and out of it frequently during the day. Once you have recognized this state, the goal is to increase and expand its occurrence so that it functions during *all* of your waking moments. You will do this with the use of competing responses (presented in subsequent chapters) and a search for the complete truth.

First, you must be able to recognize these Ego-Neutral moments. To help you achieve this recognition, we will look at several scenarios. Hopefully, in at least one of them, you will see yourself.

- Imagine yourself intensely focused upon a task. This could be any task: target practice, tennis, sewing, scrubbing a floor, studying for a test. Your thoughts are not upon yourself. Instead, they are upon an activity, which is external to you. After the task has been completed, your thoughts may return to a more self-centered, Ego-Defensive direction (e.g., I can't wait for other people to see what I have done!, or I really beat everyone on that!). During the task, however, you are in an Ego-Neutral mode, since your thoughts are involved with something outside of yourself. During that time, you are not thinking about how special you are or how special others will think you are. Instead, you are engrossed in skillfully performing a series of actions. Perhaps you are trying to show improvement over your previous performance of this activity. Acquiring mastery of a skill can be an Ego-Neutral goal.

- Recently, I attended a concert where someone played an accordion. This is not my favorite instrument. Normally I would have let my mind wander onto some of the

11

projects in which I was engaged or upon issues that concern me or maybe just think about shopping. This time, however, I stayed in the present moment and watched the performer and instrument. For the first time, I wondered about the mechanics of the instrument. How could they sustain the tune for so long before reversing the direction of the bellows? How were the bellows constructed to allow this to happen? How did the little pegs mechanically function? How did playing on the keyboard produce the sound? My concentration was upon something outside myself and could not in anyway benefit or harm me. I was completely Ego-Neutral.

- If you don't have a cat, imagine that you have one. When you affectionately call to it, occasionally the cat will come to you, but frequently it disregards you. Do you feel angry when the cat ignores you? Are you enraged because the cat disobeys you? Are you upset if the cat struggles to escape your embrace? If you answered "no" to these questions, you are relating to the cat in an Ego-Neutral way. (If you answered "yes," you are in Ego-Defensive mode. Also, you have no business owning a cat.)

  ✓ Do you care what that cat is thinking about you? Are you wondering if that cat thinks your hair looks terrible? Are you wondering if that cat finds your pimples repulsive? Are you wondering if that cat thinks you are fat? Do you want that cat to think you are popular? Do you want that cat to think you are smart? Do you want that cat to think you are cool? Do you want that cat to admire you in any way? Do you want that cat to envy you? Are you angry at the cat when it won't play with you? Are you asking yourself, "How can I get that cat to like me?" A "no" answer to these questions verifies that you are still in Ego-Neutral mode.

✓ If you answered "yes," ask yourself: What good would it do me if this cat *did* admire me? How would I feel if this cat said that I'm a loser? How would it change the way I feel about myself?

✓ A person who can relate to the cat in an Ego-Neutral way accepts the cat as it is. He does not impose self-serving expectations upon the animal. He can enjoy the cat without wondering what it thinks of him. He does not feel rebuffed when the cat ignores him. He feeds the cat and cares for it without feeling that he is unfairly burdened in the relationship. He does these things because he wants to, without any expectation of exchange.

✓ For a person in Ego-Neutral mode, neither negative nor positive opinions that the cat might have held toward him influenced **the way he felt about that cat *or* about himself.**

✓ In order to fully test being Ego-Neutral in real life, you *must assume* that admiration or censure coming from other people will influence you as much as admiration or censure coming from that cat.

✓ Now ask yourself some questions about the cat. What color are its eyes? How much does it weigh? Has it been eating enough? Does it seem sick? Asking questions of this nature requires at least a minimal level of curiosity about something or someone other than you.

• Now substitute a person you know for the cat, and ask yourself the same questions that you have just asked pertaining to your relationship with the cat. You do not feel cheated when the person fails to return your affection stroke for stroke. Furthermore, you have demonstrated that it is possible to find enjoyment with a person who does not necessarily return your affection.

- A mild level of curiosity is the attention that you should be directing toward others. When your attention is focused on others without expecting something in return, you are not thinking about yourself. This is an undiluted Ego-Neutral state.

- Think of your best friend. Why are you friends? Is it because you hate the same people? If much of your time together is spent criticizing, ridiculing and invalidating others, you are in Ego-Defensive mode. This is not a healthy basis for friendship. If your time together is spent in mutually enjoyable activities or in achieving a common goal (without competing with each other), you are in Ego-Neutral mode.

- Now imagine that your job performance is being criticized. This can be very upsetting. However, fear over keeping your job and surviving financially is not the same thing as feeling insulted because someone says your work isn't good enough. In Ego-Neutral mode, you may be able to determine if there is any truth in the criticism and correct the deficiency. In Ego-Defensive mode, you will tend to focus your attention on attacking the critic or unproductively defending a performance that may be truly deficient.

- You may find yourself feeling shy and awkward when you are in the presence of people who are the same age as or older than you are. This is a state of Ego-Defense. You are concerned with being excluded and with what you can do to be acceptable. In contrast, when you are with younger people, these feelings may be replaced with an interest in things other than yourself and how you feel. With these younger people, you are able to concentrate on topics and activities outside yourself. You feel at ease. You are not concerned about being judged by them. This is the state of Ego-Neutrality. Do not confuse this with the Ego-Defensive situation, in which an older person, while near younger people, may resort to controlling, manipulating behavior. The latter behavior is *not* Ego-Neutral!

- Each day, take one scenario from the chapter entitled Ego-Defensive vs. Neutral Examples. Have someone (coach) read the scenario and the triggering event, or imagine that someone is initiating the scenario. First, react with your immediate, impulsive response. Then, have your coach read the scenario again. This time you should respond with your own Ego-Neutral handling of the situation.

Guidelines for an Ego-Neutral existence:

- **It is imperative that you be more concerned with what you genuinely think of others than with what you think others think of you.**

- **Maintain a mild level of curiosity about the people and events and things around you.**

- **Look outward, not inward.**

- **Be objective!**

It is essential that you strive to function in an Ego-Neutral mindset every day throughout your life – Beginning Now!

Until you are habitually in an Ego-Neutral frame of mind, before going to bed, review the events of each day. Did you regress into an Ego-Defensive mode? What triggered the relapse? If you could replay the incident, how would you do it now?

Note: Some people appear to approach the state of Ego-Neutrality described above, in that they are not consciously aware of any concern about what others think of them. Still, they persist in trying to evoke in others responses such as affection, approval, agreement, annoyance, anger, despair, guilt and self-hatred. Others indulge in vandalism. What have they gained from this? They have destroyed something of value, and at the same time they have gained nothing. This is simply bullying and invalidating others. They are in Ego-Defensive-Victor-Wannabe mode. They gain nothing beyond smugness and a possible brief elevation of adrenaline. At the same time, they have destroyed a potential friendship. They have removed from the future a possible ally. They have acquired an enemy. They have everything to lose and nothing to gain with such behavior.

Unless it is a matter of self-defense, *do not engage in destructive acts of any kind!* To do this defines you as an Ego-Defensive Victor and poisons your surrounding environment. Accept others as they are. Allow them to go forward, with their lives, *unimpeded.* After all, that's what you want them to do for you!

Isn't it?

Always Be Honest With Yourself

At first you must make a conscious effort to be aware of the reasons for your behavior. (This is the search for complete knowledge.) Ask yourself, "Why am I doing what I am doing? Why do I behave this way?"

There are no right or wrong answers (judged by someone else). There are only honest answers and only you know if they are really honest. Also, you may have more than one reason for thinking or doing something. Try to be aware of all of the reasons.

Are you being nice to someone because you think that you will attain some advantage if he likes you?

Are you being nice to someone because you are friends and you really like that person?

Are you able to see both appealing and unappealing aspects in the same person and still accept him, warts and all?

Are you being nice to someone as a matter of principle, because your only other option would be rudeness and you don't want to hurt his feelings?

At a football game, do you cheer because everyone else is, so it must be the right thing to do?

Are you cheering at a football game because you are genuinely caught up in the excitement?

Are you attending the game because you like football?

Are you attending the game because your friends are attending?

(Note: This can be a perfectly valid reason. Just don't deceive yourself that you went to the game for another reason.)

Do you dislike and ridicule someone because he has been unkind to you?

Do you dislike and ridicule someone only because all of your friends dislike and ridicule that person?

Do you smoke because you enjoy the taste it leaves in your mouth and the burning sensation in your airways?

Do you smoke because all of your friends do?

Do you smoke because you think it makes you look cool?

Do you have an opinion simply because peer pressure says you **must** have that opinion? Do you honestly agree? Do you honestly disagree? Do you honestly not care?

Ask yourself, "If I *didn't know* how my friends felt about this matter, would I *still* feel this way?"

Ask yourself, "If my friends didn't do [activity – you fill in the blank], would I still want to do it?"

Are you feeling hopeless about your life getting better because your family or peers say that the cards are somehow stacked against you, so even trying to improve yourself is a waste of time and effort?

Over time, you will become more aware of just how much *you* **have allowed others to control your feelings, perceptions and behavior.** *Paradoxically, you have done this in the hope of gaining control and influence over those people.* Whenever you let this happen, you actually abandon *all* of your power and all of your ability to make *yourself* happier. You give your power to someone else. You become a slave.

Then ask yourself, "Do these other people really like me more because I am doing what I think they like instead of doing **what I really like?**"

Why are you twisting yourself into a pretzel trying to think and feel the way you *think* that others feel? Instead, you could be effortlessly thinking and feeling your own thoughts and feelings. For all you actually know, people *might* like you better as yourself. A genuine you is far better than a counterfeit anyone else.

Two more points on honesty:

- When you are wrong, recognize it, willingly admit it to yourself *and to others* and apologize, if appropriate. How do you apologize? You say, "I apologize." While you may hope that your apology will be accepted, that is not the goal. The goal is to assume accountability for whatever you did and to acknowledge your error to the injured person. The injured person does not have to accept your apology to make your effort a success. It became a success when you said you were sorry.

- When you are criticized, try to see both sides of the issue. It is entirely possible that the criticism is justified. View it as a learning opportunity, not as an insult, and thank the critic for calling your attention to the shortcoming. This transforms a negative evaluation of yourself into a helpful communication *and* guides you in self-improvement. Try it. It can actually feel pretty good.

Be Reliable

Being reliable means:

- Delivering what you have agreed to deliver.
- Doing what you have said you will do.
- Being on time.
- Being where you say you will be.
- Keeping your promise.

It's that simple.

You dislike it when other people fail to meet these standards. This is because when someone else violates any of the above items, they have stolen something from you. They have stolen time from your life, or they have diminished your ability to achieve the outcome you desired by using an alternate plan. Why should they accept such failures from you?

If you are reliable, you are more likely to be trusted and less likely to be shunned.

Be Polite

Politeness is the positive side of not being rude. It is the positive side of not being unkind.

- You know when someone has been unkind to you. ***Don't be unkind to others!***

- You know when someone has been rude to you. ***Don't be rude to others!*** (Even when you are kidding, your target may think you are serious.) Politeness enhances fair exchange. Rudeness closes the door to any further communication on the disputed subject.

- Being polite does not mean succumbing to the orders of a dominator, although it is easy to slip into that strategy. It is indeed possible to be polite and still say no. You can have 'No' mean 'No' without screaming '***NO! NO! NO! DAMN IT!***' For example:

  ✓ No, I'm not comfortable doing that, and these are the reasons why.

  ✓ No, I'm just not comfortable doing that, and I don't want to discuss those reasons right now.

  ✓ No, but I'm willing to compromise and do part of what you want.

  ✓ I'm sorry, but I just don't have the time right now.

  ✓ I'm sorry, I don't have the time right now, but I could do it later. *State a specific time and follow up by honoring your commitment.*

  ✓ No. I feel like I'm the one who is doing all of the giving, and you are the one who is doing all of the taking. It's not that I don't want to help you, but we need to find some way to balance our relationship. This means fair exchanges, so that sometimes you do what I ask.

✓ No.

- It is important to acknowledge the existence of others. This can be done as you pass them in the hall or on the street with a simple nod of the head, smile or wave. You don't have to like someone or want to spend time with him in order to acknowledge his existence.

- If you are consistently polite, you will not be driving people away from you.

- It is especially important to be polite to members of your immediate family! Some people say that home is where you can be yourself. Don't use that place to be your worst self. Always be the person that you want non-family members to see. There is enough rudeness out in the street. Home should be a sanctuary from such stress.

  ✓ Remember your goal is to **become** Ego-Neutral, not just to pretend to be Ego-Neutral in front of people you are trying to impress. Being polite in your own home will strengthen the habit of being in Ego-Neutral mode everywhere. Family members are the people most frequently and easily accessible to you. Therefore, they afford the best opportunity to practice until Ego-Neutrality becomes a firm habit.

  ✓ Usually the home affords the best opportunity to improve your skills of compromise and fair exchange.

  ✓ See above on how to say "No" politely.

Be Neat and Clean

People will not want you near them if you smell bad. (That's a no-brainer!)

Perfume *cannot* substitute for the omission of soap and water on your clothes and on yourself. Also, too much perfume is as offensive as not enough bathing. Show some restraint when you splash on the fragrance. It makes some people physically ill.

Bathing and then putting on dirty, smelly clothes doesn't help either.

Brush your teeth at least twice a day and brush your tongue and roof of your mouth while you're doing it.

Do not use extreme clothing and hairstyles to blatantly call attention to yourself. Why? See the chapter about calling attention to yourself. Look up the word "blatantly" in the dictionary, if you don't know what it means.

Shocking people with a bizarre appearance says a lot about you, but nothing you would want to hear. Why? See the chapter about not being a show-off.

Being neat (as well as clean) shows a sufficient level of interest in caring for yourself. It also demonstrates an acceptable level of mental as well as physical health. You don't have to spend a lot of money to have a satisfactory or agreeable appearance.

Don't Be a Show-Off

Calling attention to yourself by appearance or behavior looks to others as the act of a greedy, selfish, needy person. It is an obvious attempt to manipulate a response in others. They will tend not to trust you. Don't be a show-off. Squelch the impulse. Don't do it!

Years ago, I knew an army officer who was born and grew up in Kansas. This reality was not enough for him. He constantly affected a British inflection. What was to be gained from this pretense? He clearly revealed his need to elevate his status. He was obviously dissatisfied with his real self. His intent was to appear cultured and commanding. Instead, he achieved the opposite, looking pretentious, needy and ridiculous.

People (especially young people) in a group sometimes indulge in attention-getting behaviors. They do this by being unnecessarily noisy and by trying to impress others with what a very good time they are having. If the good time were genuine, there would be no need (and no attempt) to impress others. An Ego-Neutral person would be indifferent to what others thought of him.

Some people enjoy deliberately shocking others with inappropriate behavior, speech or appearance. This is typical Ego-Defensive-Victor behavior. It is disrespectful and abusive. If you experience any significant personal growth, you may well look back on such occasions with regret and embarrassment.

By contrast, admiring or pointing out the good points of others is encouraged. (We are not talking flattery, which is manipulation.) Do this only if you feel that there is honestly something to validate. When you are focused on the good points of others, you are not thinking excessively about yourself. Instead, your focus is outward rather than inward. This is central to becoming Ego-Neutral.

Self-Improvement and Goals

Self-improvement gives you the knowledge that you actually *can* improve. You will know that you are capable of starting from knowing nothing about a skill to, in time, becoming a master of that skill.

It allows you to experience the satisfaction and pride that comes from mastering a skill. Do you remember the first time you rode a bicycle without the training wheels and without someone helping you to balance?

Do you remember the first time you drove a car? The resulting thrill of accomplishment and power can be among life's major moments.

Successfully overcoming challenges gives you the self-confidence that you *can* confront *other* areas as a beginner and eventually become an expert.

It increases your comfort level in the face of uncertainty and the unknown (and believe me, life is mostly uncertainty and unknowns).

You acquire self-discipline.

You experience the satisfaction of seeing how much you have improved.

What skill should you learn? Just about anything, with the following restrictions: Select an activity that will add positive value to your existence and will not remove value from the existence of others.

Carpentry

Cooking

Sewing

Skateboarding

Computer programming

Many of the activities are mentioned in the chapter on expanding your contacts with other people.

Don't waste your time on video games or computer solitaire. Once you turn off the computer, you are back into real life. And all you have to show for it is lost time and possible carpal tunnel syndrome.

Don't spend your time hacking or creating computer viruses. This is obvious Ego-Defensive Victor behavior. It is unworthy of you. It is an attempt to control others, by infecting their computers with viruses (and in the process, ruining things for innocent people). It is also an attempt to prove that others cannot control you (by hacking into things they have forbidden you to access). Also, it is illegal. Spend your time *constructively*.

Academic performance is *definitely* something you need to improve upon, even if you think you are already good. Remember you do *not* have to like or enjoy or agree with a subject in order to understand it.

As you undertake these self-improvement goals, do not measure yourself against other people. *The only person you ever have to be better than is yourself.* Delight in how far you have come.

Self-improvement requires beneficial, constructive goals. These should be long-term, intermediate and immediate. For example, the ultimate long-term goal might be to become a brain surgeon. Intermediate goals would include going to college and doing well in courses, especially science courses, then going to medical school. Another intermediate goal, depending upon your level of education, would be to finish high school. An immediate goal would be to study for tomorrow's test. Another immediate goal would be to clean your room. This is because it is easier to organize your thoughts if you are not immersed in clutter.

It is important to live a goal-driven life. Goals provide the framework for engaging in constructive competing responses. In this way, goals help you to avoid drifting back into the Ego-Defensive mode. It is important to live a goal-driven life even if you are not engaged in the Ego-Neutral program. Life, without some goal to attain, is meaningless and tedious.

I once knew a middle-aged woman who came from a prosperous family. Her parents bought her a house and gave her just enough allowance to permit her to live frugally. Her father owned a residential real-estate company. She trained to be an appraiser. Her life consisted of going to her father's office every day and reading the morning paper. She waited there day after day for the occasional appraising task to appear. When I asked if she would be interested in selling real estate, she replied, "Oh, it's too much of a headache." When I asked if she would be interested in going back to college and training for something, her reply was, "Oh, it's too much of a headache." When I asked if she would be interested in doing volunteer work, her reply was (you guessed it!), "Oh, it's too much of a headache." By her own admission, she was lonely. She wanted to date, but had no contact with eligible men. Her life was boring and had no prospect of becoming interesting because of her refusal to reach beyond herself for something worthwhile.

Without a goal to pursue, you tend to rot. Choose goals that will advance your life!

Meeting People

If this book is about not caring what others think about you, why should you care about meeting people? While wanting to be popular is an Ego-Defensive desire, having compatible companions can enormously enrich your life. Not every acquaintance, even when you share some common interests, will become a friend. Finding a friend is a numbers game. This is why it is important to meet and interact with as many people as possible. In this way, you improve the likelihood of finally connecting with someone who has compatible interpersonal "chemistry." No matter how polite and non-judgmental you are, some people will not like you and some people will actively dislike you. Their response is due either to their immersion in pecking-order mentality or to incompatible interpersonal chemistry or some combination of both.

Adults, for example, can join civic organizations, such as the Chamber of Commerce and Rotary. They can also participate in church functions or other volunteer community projects. They can take dancing lessons.

Students can participate in extra-curricular activities: band, orchestra, chorus, drama club, debate, newspaper, sports, yearbook, etc. In various classes, find people to study with and then actually study. Initially, it might be helpful to get a fresh start away from school. **That way you will less likely to revert to the Ego-Defensive mode.** You will also be meeting people who do not have habitual ways of behaving toward you.

You will discover that people of all ages and interests can be excellent companions. Do *not* consider them second-choice companions. *All* people with whom you enjoy sharing your thoughts, interests and activities are *top-choice* companions.

Here are a few places to meet people: church and community choir, chess clubs, volunteer work, political campaigns, Civil Air Patrol, classes at the local community college, community theater (You don't have to be the star. Someone is always needed to paint sets, etc.), church youth groups, gun clubs. Get a part-time job. Work in a soup kitchen. Join a computer club or a garden club or do volunteer work for battered women. Join a kennel club if you have a dog. Help at the hospital. Ask the reference librarian at your local library for lists of community activities and special interest groups.

Seriously consider getting involved in golf, tennis and/or bridge. Why? Participating in these activities is an excellent way to meet people throughout your entire life *starting now.* Take lessons if you have no way to learn informally. See the reference librarian at your public library to learn if there are local groups that sponsor beginners in these activities and perhaps provide low-cost lessons.

This should be a major period of exploration for you. You will be implementing a new way emotionally to perceive and interact with people. You should also be exploring new activities in addition to continuing some activities that you already enjoy. Why? You may find there are other activities that you enjoy more than the ones you know now. You have made *major* gains if you find a combination of activities you enjoy, plus companions with whom you can share your interests. This is what makes life good!

OK. You know about the Ego-Neutral state, and you are at the event and all of these people are around you, and you feel just as awkward and out of place as you did before you ever read this book. Now what do you do?

Remember, others are *not* interested in hearing much, if anything, about you. They are interested in performing the activity and perhaps discussing the activity or discussing other things that are on *their* minds. *Do not, for even a moment, assume that others are interested in you!*

- Remember the feeling of Ego-Neutral. Your focus should not be on you. Your focus should not be on invoking an emotional response in others. Your focus should be on others, and on interests and activities that you have in common with them.

- Talk about yourself only if you are answering a direct question.

- You might try brief questions about the activity or about the people around you. You might ask about the activity that is the focus of the group. Or you might ask someone how long they have been in the group, what they think of the group, etc. You do this by developing genuine interest and curiosity about the people and things around you. This does NOT have to be intense, brow-wrinkling curiosity. Mild curiosity will do very nicely. They will answer you. If another question comes to mind through your natural curiosity, ask that question also. And so on.

- You can also sit quietly and observe the people around you. Be interest*ed*, rather than interest*ing*.

- You can also participate in the activity or in some related activity. This will help keep you from feeling (and looking) as awkward as you otherwise might feel (and look). Engaging in some activity helps you to focus on something outside of yourself and on something other than what people *might* be thinking about you. This is an example of the competing response. Helping with cleanup, for example, is always welcome and establishes you as a thoughtful contributor. Ask someone how you can help. This will keep you from appearing too pushy in a new environment and still give you the appearance of being someone who is eager to contribute.

- After a few events, if you feel you need more specific help on what to do among strangers, read the book *How to Win Friends and Influence People* by Dale Carnegie, or take the course. The book is just as valid today as when it was initially written. Although the title could be construed as a method of manipulating people, the book is actually focused on enabling people to be more comfortable with each other. It can provide you with strategies for breaking the ice.

- Remember, if you are unfamiliar with some of these activities: It is OK to admit that you are a beginner and to ask for help. Many people really enjoy being counselors or coaches or trainers. *Remember*: In a new situation *(or any situation!)*, it is OK to admit you are uncomfortable or don't know what to do, and then to ask for guidance.

- You are also a beginner in establishing this new type of relationship with others. You may revert to the behavior of judging yourself.

  ✓ *Don't beat yourself up* if you feel you have been less than perfect! Cut yourself some slack. You are new at this.

  ✓ Remind yourself of how Ego-Neutral feels. Then apply it.

  ✓ When going into a new situation, ask yourself, "If they don't like me, what is the worst thing that can happen? Will they cut off my head? Will I be banished forever if I fail to immediately endear myself to everyone? If I annoy someone, will that person necessarily hate me forever?" (The answers to the questions are usually "*No*".) Since the worst won't happen, you must continue exposing yourself to these situations until you have improved your comfort level.

  ✓ Keep trying!

Section 1 Quiz

What is a working hypothesis?

From your own experience, give an example of a working hypothesis.

In your own words, how does being Ego-Neutral differ from being Ego-Defensive? If you can't answer this, read Concepts (Section 2).

From your own life, recall specific incidents in which you were Ego-Defensive.

From your own life, recall specific incidents in which you were Ego-Neutral.

Why is it important to be polite?

Find an instance today in which you were polite.

Find an instance today in which you were not polite.

Find an instance today in which you were downright rude!

Why is it important to be reliable?

Find an instance today in which you were reliable.

Find an instance today in which you were unreliable.

Were you a show-off today?

If yes, why? What did you gain from it?

Do you still feel good about it?

What can you realistically do to meet new people?

Are you doing it?

If no, why aren't you?

Have you defined any kind of attainable, desirable goal?

Are you working toward attaining the goal?

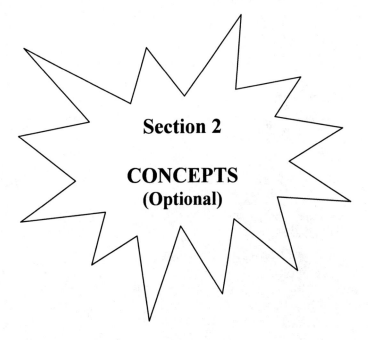

Section 2

CONCEPTS
(Optional)

What is Ego-Defensive
and
Why Are So Many People That Way?

Let us define ego as the conscious part of the personality. It perceives and reacts to the external environment to increase the chance of individual survival. It evaluates itself as surviving or not surviving, prevailing or failing. Excessive concern with pecking-order issues results in a chronic state of Ego-Defense.

The term "pecking order" was derived from the naturally occurring social hierarchies in herds, packs, flocks, or other groupings. For example, in a flock of chickens there is only one who is dominant over the entire flock. It can peck any other bird in the flock without fear of retaliation or defeat. The second from the top can safely peck any bird in the flock other than the acknowledged leader. The third from the top can safely peck any bird other than the two who are above it in the pecking order. And so on, until you reach the last bird in the pecking order. Any other bird belonging to that flock can peck this unfortunate creature. It cannot peck any other bird and in very short order doesn't even try. It succumbs to its social position, but does not leave the flock because it is biologically programmed to exist with other members of its species. Also, it doesn't know of any alternative flocks. Nature has, thus, supplied a biological basis for the Ego-Defensive pattern of emotional response and subsequent behavior.

Pecking order behavior has biological advantages for the species, though not necessarily for the individual, unless that individual is number-one in his group.

- First, it guarantees that only the physically strongest will reproduce in significant numbers. This is essential when living in the wild, where every creature is potentially some other species' meal. The head of the pecking order is the strongest, most physically fit and most aggressive individual in the social group. The head of the pecking order gets the first choice of food, sexual partners, etc. In this way, offspring descend from the strongest, most survival-prone members of the group.

- Second, it imposes order upon the social group. The absence of chaos and the assignment of roles allows attention to be focused on activities that enhance survival of the group, such as hunting or watching for predators. For example, female lions do the hunting, with the best hunter leading the hunt.

The biologically-based pecking order is expressed in humans through the following two points of view:

- What we think others think of us (stronger or weaker).

- How we see ourselves in relation to others (stronger or weaker).

The tendency is to see yourself as you think others see you. To perceive yourself as higher in the pecking order produces a feeling of pride and power. To perceive yourself as lower in the pecking order produces a feeling of shame. Shame is quickly followed by rage (directed either toward others or toward your self) or despair.

Ego-Defense can take two forms: Victor or Victim. This is derived from the person's self-perceived position in the pecking order. Sometimes the same person will alternate roles, depending on the circumstances. He will be a victor/dominator/abuser when he can get away with it, and a helpless, unaccountable victim when he cannot be a victor. It all boils down to controlling or being controlled. You are defined as victor or victim by the form of behavior that you most frequently exhibit.

You tend to carry your habitual position in the pecking order from group to group, sometimes for the rest of your life. It doesn't matter how many fresh starts you make or how many new groups you access. A small inner voice is there, every waking minute, to remind you of what you really think you are – a loser. The new group may not know who you are, but *you* know who you are! Eventually, the new group will take you at your own self-evaluation.

In the rest of this book, we will sometimes use the term, ED (pronounced eee-dee), to mean Ego-Defensive.

People are Ego-Defensive because sometimes (especially initially!) it can feel very, very good! There is the warm empowering glow arising from group acceptance after you thought that you might be excluded. There is delight in being the center of attention. There is the feeling of energy and power you experience after overcoming an opponent. There is the exuberance of victory. And from all of this is the sense of becoming bigger.

If you are an Ego-Defensive Victim, after enduring an existence of feeling judged and humiliated, it is an enormous relief to find people who *seem* not to judge you (you have found another, friendlier flock!), who seem to accept you and maybe even seem to approve of you. It is warm! It is safe! It is happy! And you just *cannot* get enough of it! This warm-fuzzy experience occurs because you finally feel accepted. You no longer feel like an outsider. When you are with these accepting people, you feel able to accept yourself.

This experience is like being on drugs. At first, you love it because you feel high. Later, you need the companionship of these people in order to feel normal. Only when people seem to accept you are you able to feel right about yourself. Without the acceptance of others, you feel lost and diminished.

Frequently, group members that have accepted you have the same self-esteem issues that you have. Outsiders don't want to remain outside and so they are attracted to others who also feel excluded. When enough of these people join together, they are no longer outsiders. You and they are now insiders: members of a supportive group. This type of group frequently is not engaged in productive activities. Members of such groups tend to spend a lot of time together drinking, doping, partying, ridiculing or resenting or harming selected outsiders and killing time. They do this because it is less painful to be bored or unhappy in the company of other people who seem to be accepting than to be bored or unhappy alone. They are using you, just as you are using them: to increase their own feeling of self-acceptance. Their approval is a drug for you and your approval is a drug for them – nothing more and nothing less.

Over time, this other-dependent self-acceptance will block your personal growth. You will spend a great deal of unproductive time with people who are using you like a drug. Instead, you could be using that time to improve your skills and establish contact with other people who might introduce you to more constructive activities and circumstances. You will find yourself limiting your interests to those of the people who appear to accept you. You will attempt to think and behave more and more as the others appear to think and behave. You will do this to reduce the possibility of incurring disapproval of the group, or you will do it eagerly, compulsively, getting higher and higher on the warmth and excitement of belonging.

Congratulations!

You've just sold your soul for a pat on the head!

- You have abandoned pursuing your own interests.
- You have ceased thinking for yourself.

- You have replaced your own thoughts and feelings and goals and sense of right and wrong with values you *think* are held by the people who *appear* to accept you.

- Even though you finally have been accepted into a group, you may begin to wonder why your life seems so stale and unfulfilling – but you won't know what to do. *If you have reached this point, following the program in this book can help you become Ego-Neutral.*

The condition of Ego-Defensive Victor is more correctly expressed as ED Victor Wannabe. This is because there is room for only one at the top. Rarely does a person reach this elevated state. Once it is attained, the position must constantly be defended because the Wannabes will continue to strive for it. For the sake of brevity, the word Wannabe will not be used frequently, but keep in mind that ED Victors are in a constant stressful state of aggression or defense. They are driven, not so much by desire to win, as they are by fear of failure. "Offense is the best defense" is the motto.

If you are in Ego-Defensive Victor mode, you habitually engage in controlling, manipulative or bullying behavior. Initially, when you succeed in this strategy, you feel much stronger and safer. Your constant goal is to make others fear you or need you and most of all – obey you. Here, again, this behavior arises from the need to feel safe, and eventually, it becomes a habit. You have concluded (and now believe) that if you can control enough, maybe someday you will be and feel safe enough. You also feel that the more you have, the stronger you are. Thus, you spend your life collecting tokens of your strength. It is much more difficult to persuade an Ego-Defensive Victor than to persuade an Ego-Defensive Victim that detaching from the pecking order is satisfying. This is because every time you have successfully controlled or, without negative consequences to yourself, harmed another human being, you feel that you have won. What have you won? Safety? Peace of mind? Respect? No. You have merely scored another point in the pecking-order game, which **you *believe* is the only game in town**. Naturally, you do not recognize this as a belief. You **"know"** it is a fact.

How much do you need to control in order to feel safe? There is *never* a feeling of enough safety. There will *always* be the compulsion to control more. You will always need to prove to yourself, and others, just how much you can get away with. This is based on the hope that when you are above the rules of law that you cannot be controlled or judged by others. Each time you control an outcome, you are reassured that you are still winning.

You are totally oblivious to the notion that you can achieve your goals through civility, sharing, fair exchange and negotiation, rather than through domination and theft. The thing you steal is not necessarily money. By forcing or manipulating others, you have stolen someone's freedom of choice. By making another feel inadequate, you have stolen his self-respect. By coercing another into supporting an issue with which he disagrees, you have stolen his integrity.

Ego-Defensive Victors live only to accumulate money or power or both. You have basically become a cheat and a thief. You are constantly attempting to control people or take things that are not truly yours to control or own. In economics this is known as an *externality*. This means that the person who benefits from a situation is not the person who pays the price. You count your successes only by what you are able to amass or by what you are able (with impunity) to damage. When you are young, you are a gang member or school bully, demanding respect you have not earned. When you are older, you may become a tyrant whenever you can get away with it. You see this in the abusive spouse and abusive parent. You see this in corrupt politicians. You see this in rogue CEOs who, without a second thought, in their quest for ego-embellishment, have destroyed companies and thousands of lives and are now engaged in destroying our country by sending our jobs offshore. People like these have caused more damage to the citizens of this country than terrorists have a chance of doing. And still, it is not enough to satisfy them. ED Victors are consumed with resentment when unable to attain their goals. ED Victors view the suffering they have caused with complete indifference, or with pride – using the destruction of others as evidence of the strength and safety they want to always have. ("I don't get ulcers, I give them!")

ED Victors are obsessed with acquiring power and tokens of power. This addictive behavior is an attempt to fill a gaping, bottomless hole. This hole can never be filled. The more you put into it, the larger it becomes. There is not enough money, physical attractiveness, popularity or alcohol; there are not enough drugs, houses, expensive clothes, boats, airplanes, trophy wives, successful husbands, prestigious jobs or influential friends to fill that hole. There will always be someone who has more of what you want. If power-addicted people are ever to attain a state of personal comfort, the hole, itself, must shrink. Detaching from the pecking order can cause this hole to become smaller and then vanish.

You are embroiled in a game that no one can truly win. A few ED Victors eventually reach the top of the mountain. You may be one of them. You will have accumulated all of the power and control you have spent a lifetime coveting and pursuing. You will have achieved your heart's desire, only to discover the reality is hollow, unfulfilling, disappointing. Then the question confronts you: "Is this all there is?"

At this point, there are five possible directions for the remainder of your life:

- Compulsively continue to control and accumulate. You feel unable to do otherwise because you have made a lot of enemies. There is usually someone in the wings waiting for a chance to steal from you or bring you down. Also, you don't know how to do anything else. Daily, something must be conquered or you fear you are losing. You need to realize that you are in a game that you can never win.

- Abuse drugs and alcohol in an attempt to feel good for the moment. Winning the pecking-order game has not generated a stable sense of well-being. Chemicals offer a shortcut to a more enjoyable emotional state – at least temporarily. The downside is that when the chemically induced good feeling fades, you frequently feel worse than you did before. Over time, excessive use of these substances can degrade your ability to function in the everyday world. Also, you are flirting with permanent brain alterations.

- In a controlling role, engage in less selfish (e.g., volunteer) activities. Still needing to be the head of the committee, the president of the club, the chief event organizer, the star of the theater production.

- Pursue activities that you enjoy for the sake of the activity. This is a move toward becoming Ego-Neutral.

- Transform to Ego-Neutral.

Within the past decade, I encountered a man who, to the point of being a caricature, embodied the qualities of ED Victor. He was a retired senior officer of an international energy-related company. He went through life grabbing and snatching and taking and never saying *please* or *thank you*. He would not be able to recognize a genuine relationship if it walked up and shook hands with him. His courtship strategy was to attempt to grope me, and then inquire if I had a vibrator or did videos of intimate acts. I never felt so close to date rape in my life. While eating in a restaurant that had no bar, he made a trip to the trunk of his car for his emergency stash of martinis. His breakfast was two Bloody Marys. When he wasn't making sexually suggestive remarks, he was complaining that his first wife turned his children against him; his second wife was an adulterous tramp; his children were all alcoholics and drug addicts and unfit parents; his siblings were worthless parasites, and someone owed him $60,000. All he had going in his life was money. I'm not saying money is unimportant. Money is very important. Money increases your alternatives. However, money is not everything. The sad part is that this executive will never see his role in all of this. He will always blame someone else for his discontent. He is dissatisfied with his life because he has emotionally poisoned himself and everything and everyone around him. He will continue to do this because he thinks it is necessary in order to "win." Too bad! He loses! And with all that money, he could have been living a really good life!

Regardless of the type of expression of Ego-Defense (Victor or Victim), the solution is the same. Address the beliefs that are dominating you and transform your focus to Ego-Neutrality, which will be addressed in the next chapter.

Ego-Neutrality and Ego-Defense each consist of three components:

- **Perception** *(what you think others think of you). ED Victors and Victims alike think that others find them personally lacking in some important way.*

- **Emotion** *(what you feel in response when you think others have found you lacking). Both Victors and Victims constantly feel concern, shame or fear when found lacking by others. When disapproval toward an ED has been expressed, Victors feel rage at the disapproving person, while Victims feel similar rage with others and/or despair over their own failure to win approval.*

- **Behavior** *(how you act in response when you feel others have found you lacking). ED Victors strike out with whatever means is available. They attack first. They use brute force, financial reprisal, insults, and* *damage to you and people and things you hold dear. Their responses to perceived slights are all out of proportion to the magnitude of actual events. They get even! ED Victims will either continue attempting to ingratiate themselves or will withdraw from the people who found them lacking or from the social world in general. Passive-aggressive behavior is also a frequent activity for ED Victims and for ED Victors who have temporarily donned the Victim's hat. This means they will try to sabotage others while pretending to help. Additionally, the ED Victor may damage or invalidate people and things just because he can.*

What is Ego-Neutral
and
Why is That Better?

Now, let us define Ego-Neutral, also referred to as EN. This is the condition in which an individual is **not** excessively concerned with the two major pecking-order issues. In order to become Ego-Neutral, you **must** eliminate these two Ego-Defensive tendencies from your mindset:

- Comparing yourself to others (more powerful or weaker, smarter or dumber, popular or unpopular, richer or poorer, better or worse, winner or loser) and

- Worrying about how others are evaluating you (stronger or weaker, winner or loser, significant or insignificant, important or unimportant, someone or nobody).

This does not mean that the Ego-Neutral person is completely unaware of these issues. It does mean that he is not excessively concerned with them. He is more objective about himself. He looks within himself to determine his interests. He feels that the only person he needs to be better than is himself. In a previous chapter, you learned how to recognize and expand this mindset.

You may wonder why others seem so successful and happy while the world seems determined to proclaim what a loser you are. Many of these people, either through accident or cleverness, have acquired an Ego-Neutral approach to life and a genuine indifference toward being popular, admired, envied and accepted by the group. Paradoxically, this has given them an authentic self-confidence, an absence of self-consciousness and an honesty that others frequently find attractive. It is this outward, objective, Ego-Neutral focus that we discussed earlier in this book. Maintaining this objective focus will give you knowledge and ability that will serve you well, both now and for the rest of your life.

In many cultures, *physical* superiority is not always essential for the survival of the human individual. Our abilities to think abstractly and to speak serve to separate us from animals and can enable us to extricate ourselves from the pecking-order trap. **Intelligence can now be a stronger survival tool than brute force.**

The *tendency* toward pecking-order behavior is so biologically ingrained that individuals do not even recognize it and how it is influencing their self-images, perceptions of the world and life choices. A tendency is just that. It is a tendency! It is not a reflex. It is not an insurmountable instinct. **You do not have to succumb to the pecking-order mentality.** This is the entire focus of this book! People remain Ego-Defensive because they are unaware of this ingrained *tendency*. Through ignorance, they continue to be immersed in the pecking order.

What are the advantages of being Ego-Neutral?

Ego-Neutrality allows you to identify more accurately what is actually a threat. Instead of routinely treating all people as threats to be attacked or charmed or controlled, you can more clearly see what you feel, why you feel that way and, finally, what to do to resolve the discomfort. In other words, being Ego-Neutral enhances your chances of identifying the correct target and then successfully dealing with it in an appropriate way. At the same time, you avoid needlessly offending or hurting others who are not true sources of danger. It's like the difference between using a high-powered rifle versus a sawed-off shotgun to eliminate a threat in a room filled with people.

Ego-Neutrality reduces the stress in your life by allowing you to focus on real threats and dismiss imaginary threats. Once you have stopped seeing a potential enemy in every person you meet, your overall stress level will drop. The physiological components of stress will then subside and you will be healthier.

Ego-Neutrality enhances the probability that others will cooperate with you. When people sense that an Ego-Defensive person is trying to control them, the tendency is to resist, openly rebel against or impede the agenda of the ED. When others are approached by an EN for help, the tendency is to be more issue oriented, and the possibility of cooperation is improved.

Ego-Neutrality improves your chance of success because before acting, you habitually try to get full knowledge of a situation rather than proceeding on partial, biased or incorrect data. Your focus is upon gathering information in order to move toward complete truth. This is a great advantage when navigating through life.

Ego-Neutrality greatly improves your chances of having friends and associates who are also Ego-Neutral. Your life will be much easier with Ego-Neutral people in it. Why is this? ED Victors potentially bring huge amounts of opposition, attempts at control and abuse into your life. You cannot completely trust them since they will always have a hidden (or not-so-hidden) agenda of self-aggrandizement. ED Victims require large amounts of sensitivity, stroking and accommodation. Either way, if these people are in your life, you will have unnecessary difficulty in defining, focusing upon and attaining your own goals. They will constantly drain your attention and energy away from things that are important to you.

By contrast, EN people are issue-and-activity oriented rather than ego-enhancement oriented. Ego-Neutral disagreements will tend to be debates rather than disputes. It will be an exchange of information, with each party learning more of the point of view of the other. Their focus is cooperation and mutual respect, even when there is a difference of opinion. For these reasons, Ego-Neutral people tend to seek the company of other ENs and to avoid prolonged association with Ego-Defensive people whether Victim or Victor.

Ego-Neutrality greatly improves your ability to tolerate the presence of confirmed EDs. Sometimes it is not practical to immediately leave or change a situation (home, job, marriage, etc.), which is contaminated by ED manipulation. An EN orientation on your part will be of enormous benefit in dealing with ED shenanigans. Since *the major ED strategy is controlling you by controlling your feelings about yourself, you are already inoculated. This is because your feelings about yourself no longer involve the approval or disapproval of others.*

Keep in mind that an attacking ED may mistake your indifference for being intimidated. This can cause him to feel empowered by the thought that he is "winning." Then he might continue, or even escalate his attacks. When this happens, *after other EN strategies have failed*, **respond more assertively.** To leave the ED feeling victorious merely encourages his unpleasant behavior.

What about that sense of victory that occurs when you have prevailed over others? Will that be lost to you forever? No. You can experience the same rush of triumph when you have improved yourself. Don't measure yourself against others. That is distracting and keeps you mired in Ego-Defense. Always do your very best and measure yourself against the earlier you.

I may have left the impression that ED Victors, because of their determination to prevail at any cost, are the only ones who get to the top of corporations, win important political contests and become community leaders. I would like to emphasize that Ego-Neutral people are also found in these elevated positions. You don't hear about them because they are more interested in overseeing the success of their projects than in pursuing self-promoting photo-ops and public appearances.

In the previous chapter, I briefly profiled the ED Victor who superficially appeared to be a winner, but who really had nothing but money. Now I would like to profile an executive in a major Fortune 500 company. He is an Ego-Neutral Type-A personality who succeeded in a major way in corporate America. He had the drive to improve his lot in life and was able to do it in an Ego-Neutral way.

His childhood was one of poverty. His clothes were old and worn, and personal hygiene left much to be desired. The emphasis on self-improvement and education did not exist in his home. One day, he heard music from a nearby church and curiously wandered in. He was made to feel welcome and encouraged to participate in church activities. From the people he met there, he learned about the importance of neatness and cleanliness. He was encouraged to apply himself in school. He learned about Boy Scouts and joined. A few years later, in one of the groups in which he was involved, he attended an event at the local country club. He said, "I want this!"

He was able to get a college scholarship and eventually completed a doctorate in one of the sciences. His involvement with scientific work led to project management and project management led to executive positions. His strategy was always to know as much as possible about processes and situations that were his responsibility. To improve the performance of his subordinates, he focused on issues, rather than engaging in personal attacks. He was willing to assume full responsibility for his decisions and the outcomes. He had a good family life and was respected in the community. He did well in all aspects of his existence by being civil and fair and working toward win-win outcomes. This is truly a life successfully lived.

As stated in an earlier chapter, Ego-Neutrality and Ego-Defense each consist of three components:

- **Perception** *(what you think others think of you). Ego-Neutral people are aware that people may or may not like them. Rather than assuming that no one likes them, or that everyone is a threat, they take this on a case-by-case basis. They do not orient their entire lives around the possibility of being liked or disliked.*

- **Emotion** *(what you feel when you think others have found you lacking). Ego-Neutral people respond to being disliked not with rage or fear, but with indifference or with curiosity and an interest in resolving misunderstanding.*

- **Behavior** *(how you act when you think others have found you lacking). If Ego-Neutral people have caused someone loss or distress, they attempt to make it right. They may seek greater knowledge of the opponent's point of view. This could involve looking to see if some misunderstanding has occurred or attempting to discover if they have inadvertently upset someone. This is done because it is easier to be around people who aren't mistakenly upset with you. On the other hand, since Ego-Neutrals do not need the good opinion of others in order to feel good about themselves, they may choose to ignore the matter. Ego-Neutral people address issues, rather than resorting to personal attacks. They do not engage in idle negative gossip. While they may need to deal with a troublemaker, they do not seek revenge. Instead, they look for ways to reduce negative influence. In dealing with others, they strive for fair exchange. Their goal is a win-win outcome, rather than winner-take-all. The EN avoids needlessly invalidating and damaging people and things. This is because such actions would degrade his integrity and would ultimately poison the world around him and diminish the overall quality of the culture.*

Section 2 Quiz

Were you Ego-Defensive today?

Give some specific examples.

What did you gain by being Ego-Defensive?

Just before you became Ego-Defensive, what happened?

How could you have been Ego-Neutral instead?

Were you Ego-Neutral today?

Give some specific examples.

Did you choose to be Ego-Neutral over being Ego-Defensive today?

Give some specific examples.

Why did you choose to be Ego-Neutral on those occasions?

If you are confused about Ego-Neutral vs. Ego-Defensive behavior, see Appendix C. Do not read it all at once. Read three or four scenarios each day until you have a stable feeling for the two states.

Section 3

BEEN THERE!
(Optional)

My Pre-Ego-Defensive Years

I was born in 1940 and spent the first thirteen years of my life in a small town, which was surrounded by wheat and oil fields. Much of the population consisted of children or grandchildren of thrifty, hard-working Russian-German immigrants. The oil field provided greater financial affluence than normally would be expected in a town of this size and location. The citizens were ambitious and upwardly mobile, and there was a sense of civic pride that is difficult to find today. Children were expected to behave and to achieve.

When I was in the second grade, a traveling salesman came to town, selling an encyclopedia, *The Book of Knowledge*. He got a resounding "NO!" from my mother. He then went to my father's workplace and made a successful sale. On the day it arrived, I opened a volume to a two-page picture spread. It displayed the earth, moon, sun, all of the other planets in the solar system, the nearest star and the length of time it would take to arrive at each one in an airplane traveling from earth at two hundred miles an hour. I was enchanted! That day I memorized all the information on those two pages.

In the following years, I studied everything I could find on astronomy. I discovered that the planets were named after Roman gods and goddesses. This generated an interest in antiquity. Soon I was reading everything I could find on Roman and Greek mythology. After visiting William Rockhill Nelson Art Gallery in Kansas City, I developed a fascination with ancient Greek, Roman, and Egyptian artifacts plus those of other early cultures. Prior to reading *The Book of Knowledge,* I had been an indifferent student. I recall several unsatisfactory grades for reading performance. Thanks to the intellectual stimulation arising from *The Book of Knowledge*, by the sixth grade I had attained twelfth grade (high school senior) reading ability.

This was truly a positive turning point and perhaps the only positive one for a very long time. I mention the next turning point only because readers might assume it was a major factor in the ED-Victim issues that developed for me. You be the judge. It was indeed stressful, but it did not generate the pecking-order issues that eventually defined my life. It did, however, result in my abandoning my own process of thinking and feeling. Instead, I looked to my mother to define how I should think and feel toward my father and his behavior.

My father was severely alcoholic. In his early teens, he began hanging out with older people and drinking heavily. For the duration of his life, he was probably drunk more days than he was sober. It is my understanding that he had been drinking the day he killed himself.

I was eight years old when he was first shipped off for thirty days of detox and rehab. This was to have solved all of our problems. He was to have come home committed to a life of sobriety. Some staff member must have said, "When you leave here you can never drink again." The poor man interpreted this to mean that the treatment had destroyed his ability to drink. So, on the same day he was discharged, his first stop was a bar, to determine whether or not he could still imbibe. During the next ten years, there were numerous lengthy stays at Miller General, Hazelden and finally a state hospital. None were successful in motivating him toward sobriety. One doctor told my mother, "All we can do is dry him out. He has found his solution."

He wasn't a bad father. I can recall only one time when he made a half-hearted attempt to spank me. He was never physically or emotionally abusive. He was simply rarely there, so I never really knew him and he never knew me.

Every day, our overriding goal was to have him come home immediately after work and eat dinner. He rarely drank following his evening meal. The many nights he did not come home on time were filled with dread – fear that he had run off the road and was dying or dead in some ditch. I would pray, "Please God, make him come home safely just tonight! Just this one night!" Afraid that God would ignore the request if I asked for too much, I only asked for one night at a time. I really wanted to ask for forever.

I did not feel personally diminished because of my father's drinking. It never occurred to me that people would find me lacking because of **his** behavior. Unfortunately, that was not the way my mother reacted. For her, this was a distressing, embarrassing situation, which we must, at all costs, *Keep Secret!* That was a neat trick to pull off in a very small town before TV was available to distract people from local events.

Until our deep dark shameful family secret was revealed to us, my sister and I were sent to bed at seven o'clock every evening. Now, of course, we had been made full partners in the perpetual project of Keeping Daddy Sober. On nights when he came directly home and did not drink, our job was to "keep things calm." That meant no disagreements or fighting. That meant complete, unquestioning obedience to my mother. And, of course, we still had to go to bed early.

We were usually in bed when he returned home on his drinking nights. My mother would wait up in order to read him the riot act. I would lie awake and listen to the rising sound of their voices in the next room, wishing I were also allowed to say such angry things to him. In the day(s) following these episodes, the three of us would punish him with "The Silent Treatment." In the morning, as he drove me to school, I would say nothing unless he asked me a direct question (which he rarely did).

Ego-Neutral replay: Keep lines of communication open. Talk to him in the morning about things happening at school, etc. Avoid judgmental remarks or questions.

In my mother's defense, she was a victim of the time and culture. The most respectable employment options to which a woman could reasonably aspire were teacher, nurse, secretary and librarian (all low-paying jobs). If she was to do well in life, she had to marry a man who would make that good life a reality. Occasionally, an unmarried woman could become professionally successful, but people would then say, "Thank goodness she has a career, since the poor thing couldn't get a husband." Because of this cultural mindset, my mother stayed married and focused her life on manipulating her alcoholic husband into taking care of her. Being divorced carried such an enormous stigma that she refused to consider it as a possibility.

Ego-Neutral replay: Acknowledge reality. Her husband was solidly committed to drinking. Stop treating each episode of drinking as the end of the world. Recognize that divorce might be a better alternative than a family atmosphere in which every member is imprisoned from the fallout of drinking. Get training to be a teacher or nurse so there might be another source of income. This would lessen her feeling of helplessness and expand her options. Encourage the children to engage in activities outside the home so that the ongoing domestic issue is not the only thing of importance in their lives.

Alone in the Universe

During the summer, I was routinely sent out of state to visit my grandmother. She habitually visited a local faith healer two or three times a month, so I was exposed to a religious-philosophic view that was definitely not conventional. In addition to the laying on of hands, I learned of a prophecy: The world would end in 1999.

I returned home to begin fifth grade. I related this prediction to a friend, and she presented it to her class as her current-events topic. During recess, one of the girls began taunting me and calling me "Miss 1999." As I lunged at her, two other classmates grabbed me and held me back. My tormentor then contemptuously said, "Watch it, runt."

I was furious over this unprovoked attack. Outraged at the unfairness of it, I related the incident to my mother. I fully expected her to say something like, "That's all right. These other people just don't understand." I would have bet my life on it...and lost! Instead, what I got was, "What do you expect when you go around saying such silly things?" I knew that she also believed the healer was a genuine source of knowledge and power. Since she knew of my frequent exposure to his ideas, the shock resulting from her reply reverberated through the rest of my life.

I never again confided in her on any topic that left room for such disapproval and rejection. I never again discussed with her my hurt feelings and confusions. I took great pains to conceal from her any incidents in which people found me different, lacking or wrong. Fairly or not, without even verbalizing it, I concluded that if given a choice of defending me or siding with the rest of the world, she would stand with the rest of the world and throw me to the wolves. I was ten years old and all alone in a universe that did not like me.

Ego-Defensive factors in the above incident:

- The bully invading my space with an unprovoked attack.

- Mother's fear of what *her* peers would think if this out-of-the-ordinary belief became known.

- Mother's response of blaming me and only me for the incident.

- My enraged response to the unprovoked attack.

- My response to my mother's lack of support.

- My conclusion that I was somehow lacking.

- My need to conceal from my mother any disapproval from others at any time in the future.

EGO-NEUTRAL REPLAY

How Ego-Neutral attitudes might have altered the above incident:

- *If the bully had been Ego-Neutral, the incident would not have occurred (and she would not have been a bully).*

- *Long before I told my friend about the faith healer, my mother could have said, "Not everyone here will understand about Dr. K., so it would be best not to talk about him outside of our family." The incident would never have occurred.*

- *My mother could have said, "That's all right. They just don't understand." The incident would have been over for me.*

- *My mother could have said, "I wonder why that girl wanted to upset you? It probably won't happen again. Let's just see if it becomes a problem. Not everyone here will understand about Dr. K., so it would be best not to talk about him outside of our family." The incident would have been over for me.*

- *My mother could have said, "Not everyone believes the way we do. Just don't talk about it anymore. Your friends will forget what happened today." The incident would have been over for me.*

- *When I was called "Miss 1999," I could have asked, "Why do you want to hurt my feelings?" or "Have I done something to make you angry with me?" It's anyone's guess where this might have led, but my focus would have been toward objectively gathering information rather than toward enraged retaliation and self-blame. Actually, I tried to physically attack the bully because that's the response to insults I had observed in Western movies. I was exposed to these perhaps one or two times a month at Saturday matinees. Without this model of behavior, I probably would not have responded physically.*

Why Was I Excluded?

Most of my sense of isolation and deficiency stemmed, not from a single incident, but rather from a series of omissions.

Beginning in the second grade, I belonged to Brownies and, later, Girl Scouts. I also attended Sunday school class. In addition to classes in school, these activities kept me in contact with my classmates – at least the female peers.

In fifth grade, we were told to decide what instrument we wanted to play in the junior high school band. When I told my mother about this, she discouraged it, so I did not join the band. Since band practice was a frequent occurrence, it became a major catalyst for bonding with peers in a mixed-gender setting. Since I was not in the band, I did not share this experience.

At approximately the same time, square-dancing clubs began to form. I was invited to join one of them. When I approached my mother about it, her response was something to the effect, "You don't really want to do that, do you?" Thus another opportunity to bond with peers in a mixed-gender setting was lost.

I didn't understand what was going on. All I knew was that people around me seemed to enjoy being with each other, and no one seemed to want to be with me.

At the age of 10, a number of my classmates had physically matured, while I was 14 years old before having my first period. My feelings of isolation deepened by the fact that I looked about two years younger than did my contemporaries. Boys wanted to date them. No one wanted to date me. That was the biggest blow of all.

EGO-NEUTRAL REPLAY

Reducing my sense of isolation:

- *Participating in mixed-gender activities such as junior high band.*

- *Being encouraged to realize that the participation in activities is a valid end in itself.*

- *Being encouraged to not compare myself to others.*

- *Being told the only person I have to be better than is myself.*

- *Being made aware that acceptance into a group is helpful, **but not essential**, in order to experience a satisfying life.*

Please note:

Participating in group activities is ***not*** a guarantee that you will have more friends, or that your life will get better.

You ***are*** guaranteed, however, ***not*** to make new friends and ***not*** to enjoy new activities ***if you fail to participate*** in group events.

Follow-up:

When my family left Kansas at the end of my first semester of eighth grade, a surprise farewell party was given. At least 40 of my classmates, wearing their Sunday-best clothes, attended a dance at which I was guest of honor. Perhaps, after all, I was really not as ignored and isolated as I had thought. ***This demonstrates the potential gap between how you see yourself and how others might see you.***

Approximately 40 years later, while attending a reunion, two men confessed that they had experienced longtime crushes on me during those years. If only I had known!

The Downward Spiral of High School

When we moved from my Kansas home, I was determined that in the future no one would ever know what a misfit I had been (and still was). Somehow I had to be different than I had been, so that I could be respected and popular. What did *popular* mean? At that time, to me, it meant being friends with all of the popular girls and dating a boy whom the popular girls found attractive. It meant being invited to all the parties and having a date to all of the dances.

Ego-Neutral replay:

- *Being popular is not an issue. Focus is upon: being polite, neat and clean, reliable (always doing whatever I said I would do).*

- *Participating in some activities that would put me in contact with other people engaged in those same activities and seeing if friendships evolved from those acquaintances.*

- *Pursuing goals or acquiring skills that did not depend upon the approval of others in order for me to succeed.*

The payoff: Greatly reduced fear of being judged. Less focus on doing cool things with cool people would have allowed me more time to explore and participate in activities in order to determine what I truly enjoyed. Greater honesty and more forthrightness on my part would have improved my ability to communicate with my peers. It would have improved the opportunity to connect with people who actually had interests and goals similar to mine. From this, true friendship could have developed.

I began the last semester of eighth grade in the new town. Terrified, the first day I sat in the back of the room staring at the desk and my hands on the desk while the rest of the class turned to look at me and whispered. What were they saying?

Were my arms too thin? Was my hair too curly? Did I look too young? Were my clothes not right? Was my smile all wrong? How would I ever get through this day?

Ego-Neutral replay: Be an interested observer. Look at my new classmates. Smile when someone smiled at me. Wait with interest to see what new things were coming into my life. The payoff: Reduced anxiety and self-consciousness. Interest focused upon activity around me instead of being concerned about being judged.

During recess, my classmates crowded around me, asking questions. Never had I expected such friendliness and acceptance from my peers! I simply could not let them find out how marginal my social existence had been at the other place! And that decision was my downfall.

Ego-Neutral replay: Focus on where I was at that moment. Since I was new and the place was unknown to me, first of all, be a polite, interested observer. Make only positive or neutral comments about anything and anyone. The payoff:

- *Less mental stress: I would no longer compulsively try to determine what kind of person these people would like the most, so I could pretend to be that person.*

- *Possess the ability to draw a correct conclusion: These people were not friendly because of who I was or who I appeared to be. They were friendly **because that was their nature,** and as long as I was polite and interested in them, they would continue to be friendly.*

Immediately, I began hiding things that need not have been hidden. These hidden things were my spontaneous Ego-Neutral responses to my new environment. Instead, I focused on what people might want me to be. By nature, I was more of an observer than a participant. However, since my peers seemed outgoing and friendly, I felt that I should be outgoing and friendly, too. This was not a natural thing for me. I was smiling when I thought it was expected, rather than when I actually felt like it. I laughed when others laughed, even though I didn't know why they were laughing. I pretended to be enthusiastically interested in things (such as high school ball games) that didn't actually interest me.

To some extent, I felt accepted. My friends were some of the members of the in-group and so I felt that I was at least marginally a part of it. However, a sense of exclusion was still very much with me. In an attempt to prevent my new friends from knowing how left out I had felt at the other place, I pretended a worldliness that was not genuine. I expressed an interest in boys and talked as though I knew how to control them and relate to them. This was a lie. When it came to the opposite sex, I was completely clueless. Trying to be helpful, my mother said, "If you want boys to like you, you have to flirt." The only thing I knew about flirting was what I had seen in musicals at the movies – totally useless.

Although my mother was trying to be helpful in giving me pointers on how to be more attractive to boys, the conclusion I drew was that it was extremely important to be attractive to boys, and if that didn't happen, it was because there was something inherently wrong with me. I was a failure as a teenage female if there was no boy in my life. It was up to me to figure out what the boys wanted and then to become that person. Adding to my confusion on how to behave was my mother's constant monitoring of my behavior. After a party at our house, she told me I had been laughing too loudly. In other social settings, she would shoot looks at me across the room if I wasn't sitting or standing in a posture she deemed appropriate. At one point, I discovered that I felt more comfortable by admitting when a situation made me feel uncomfortable. I would say to a friend, "That gives me a complex," and we would laugh. Then my mother overheard it and said, "I want you to stop talking like that. There's nothing wrong with you, but if you keep saying you have a complex, you'll get one!"

Ego-Neutral replay: No interest in flirting, since that is an attempt to manipulate another. If there were no boys in my life, don't worry about it. Continue group activities and pursue matters of personal interest, be polite and neat and clean. Strive to be interested instead of interesting. By being interested, I could have been non-self-consciously absorbed in the world and events around me. By wanting to be interesting instead, I was focused on what the world might be thinking of me. This did not help to expand my horizons. It did not help me to meet people who shared my interests since my only interest was myself. Admitting I felt uncomfortable ("It gives me a complex") was a definite step toward Ego-Neutrality and honesty, but was aborted by my mother, who insisted that I should not admit to weakness.

I have been stalled for some time in trying to report the following. It is so painful, even from an adult perspective, to revisit this period that I have written nothing in nearly six weeks. When I reached high school, it was apparent that boys were not interested in me. The appalling fact was that for the first two years, no one wanted to date me or to dance with me at the teen dances. I continued going to the dances (unescorted), hoping each time that something would change, that some boy would want to be with me. I was queen of the wallflowers. I felt like an outcast because I did not have a boyfriend, while many of my friends did. I felt stigmatized. The lack of a boyfriend was a sign for all to know how totally unacceptable I was.

Why the boys ignored me, I still don't know. Since I had very little direct communication with them, it could not have been something I said. Was it because I looked about two years younger than did my female peers? Did some very popular girls talk unkindly about me behind my back? Was it my attention-seeking behavior as a baton twirler? Was my desperate need to be popular and important so obvious that it was repugnant to them? Was it the pecking order, with me assigned to the bottom position through group consensus?

Ego-Neutral handling of no dates: Attend dances only as a ticket-taker. Then go home. That would leave me with minimal exposure to rejection and still put me in the group setting at least briefly. If there were no boys in my life, don't worry about it. Continue group activities and pursue matters of personal interest, be polite and neat and clean.

During my junior year in high school, I went steady with a really special guy who was one year older. But it was too late. The damage had already been done. I had expected to feel better about myself if I could only go steady. Instead, once he gave me his class ring, I found him less attractive. All of a sudden his feet seemed too big! And he wanted to spend far too much time with me! I felt suffocated. I was unable to see him as a person, which was unfair to me and horribly unfair to him. I felt trapped in the relationship but was afraid to end it because I did not want to be dateless again, with the stigma that implied.

Ego-Neutral replay: Be honest about wanting to date him on weekends, but needing school nights for myself. Be willing to be alone and dateless if he did not agree to this. Find some mutually enjoyable activities beyond necking and waiting in the car while he hunted jackrabbits. Be aware that going steady is not essential for a fulfilling high school experience, but filling each day with enjoyable activities, with or without a boyfriend, is important. Identify activities that can be enjoyed without a boyfriend and participate.

Throughout high school and college, this was the pattern of my relationship with boys. First, I was only attracted to a boy if one (or even better! more than one) of my female friends said he was cute or cool or nice. I rarely had my own reasons for being attracted. I would think someone was just what I needed to make my life better. Then, as soon as he showed interest in dating me, I would find something wrong with him. He couldn't be as special as I had first thought if he was willing to date someone as undesirable as I was. There was no boy perfect enough to compensate for all of the imperfections I saw in myself.

Ego-Neutral replay of relating to significant other: Focus on mutually enjoyable activities and mutually attainable goals. Look for a relationship of cooperation and sharing instead of dominance-submission. Do not use him as a drug to try and feel better about myself. First of all, be friends. Do not date him just to have a boyfriend.

The summer following high school graduation, I experienced what perhaps has been the most satisfying romantic involvement of my life. Circumstances were such that I was actually (without realizing it) in Ego-Neutral mode. This is because during the summer between high school and college I was removed from constant exposure to the social hierarchy of high school and the social positions that seemed so unattainable by me. I knew that I would not be returning to that situation. It no longer existed for me. I was in an island of time that was free of the pecking order. There were just the two of us together, enjoying every moment of every day. Late in August, I drove him to the train and he left for the armed services. Two weeks later, I left for college. Summer had ended.

The Invisible Person

I attended a small liberal arts college several hundred miles from home. My mother helped me move into my room, then kissed me good-bye and left. As I watched her walk away, I thought, "Now I am in for it!" I no longer had my mother to tell me how to behave and think and feel. I had no certainty on the prevailing "cool" behavior. Strangers from all over the country surrounded me, and those strangers seemed very self-confident and very unimpressed with me. I was overwhelmed with apprehension and lack of direction.

Ego-Neutral replay:

- *Focus on where I was at that moment. Since I was new and the place was unknown to me, first of all, be a polite, interested observer. Make only positive or neutral comments about anything and anyone. The payoff: Less mental stress generated by trying to determine what kind of person these people would like the most, so I could pretend to be that person.*

- *Know that being "cool" is not a useful strategy. Focus is upon being polite, neat, clean and reliable.*

- *Participate in some activities that would put me in contact with other people engaged in those same activities and see if friendships evolve from those acquaintances.*

- *Pursue goals or acquire skills that do not depend upon the approval of others in order for me to succeed.*

Adding to my confusion was my mother's encouraging approval of my roommate. How could she approve of this girl? She smoked cigarettes! My mother had relentlessly lectured on the phoniness and evils of smoking. How could she possibly approve of someone who did this? Did this mean that smoking was not an issue anymore? The first thing

I learned at college was how to smoke. Why? I did it because my peers who smoked looked really self-confident and worldly. Also, someone told me that you could start conversations with guys by asking them for a light. Within a week, I was chain-smoking and continued to consume one and a half to two packs per day for the next seven years.

Ego-Neutral replay: Do not start smoking in an attempt to be more attractive. It is harmful and self-defeating. People will like you or dislike you without regard to your decision on non-smoking. Smoking may actually cause some people to avoid you since you don't smell very pleasant when this is a habit.

My day-night cycles were disrupted. I absolutely could not stay awake after lunch. So during the afternoon, when many students were in the library studying, I was taking a three-hour nap. Then, when it was time for bed, I didn't feel sleepy until after midnight. I was constantly tired and had problems with my courses. My memory was impaired, and my ability to organize the material in any meaningful way was non-existent. I barely squeaked by with C's.

Ego-Neutral replay: Force myself into a normal sleeping schedule by avoiding naps – even if it means spending the entire afternoon walking in order to stay awake. It is essential to physical health and my emotional state to stick to a normal day/night cycle. If extra sleep is needed, go to bed earlier at night.

Be involved in some activity (golf, tennis, art or other course of study involving the possibility of meeting other people) to stay awake in the afternoon, if staying awake is a problem. If staying awake is not a problem, spend the time studying.

If I had been able to retain what I studied and done well on tests, perhaps I would not have traveled down the road that eventually ended in a mental hospital. I would have, to some extent, satisfied my need to be an Ego-Defensive Victor by becoming a physician. The power and prestige that were attached to that profession would have placed my life on a more constructive course than the one that actually unfolded.

My mother thought a small college was ideal because I would not get lost in a crowd. Nice theory, but it didn't work out that way. Actually, the college was small enough that I knew most of the people at the top of the pecking order and knew that I was not one of them. I dated occasionally, but none of my dates were from the top of the pecking order either. Therefore, I viewed them as placeholders, not people. They were people to spend time with until better ones came along.

Ego-Neutral replay: View each date as worthwhile in his own right, without regard to my perception of the pecking order and his position in it.

My sense of isolation and personal deficiency is difficult to communicate. I had no female friends. I had no close male friends. In contrast to my preppy classmates, I was too thin, had unmanageable curly hair and a face marred by skin eruptions.

Everywhere I looked, I found proof of my failure as a human being. I felt inherently defective, inherently contemptible and inherently an object for ridicule. It was as though something in the very core of my being separated me from the rest of humanity.

Each morning, I stumbled out of bed and into the bathroom thinking, "I hate this place! I hate this place!" But that was not true. What I hated was myself.

Briefly, I saw the school's counselor. However, I was so ashamed of my social inadequacies I couldn't even state what was troubling me. After talking around the issue for several sessions, I stopped seeing him.

The summer between my freshman and sophomore years, I worked at the Grand Hotel on Mackinac Island. A couple of significant things transpired that summer.

First, I was realizing how angry I was with my mother. She had so ill-prepared me to be on my own. None of the things she told me to do worked: flirt, smile a lot, be friendly, be cheerful and finally, ironically, be yourself. In all of the scrutiny, evaluation and control she had imposed, how could I ever know who I was? The only thing I knew was that I had failed her and that she had failed me.

I was outraged over her hypocrisy. How could she know how I should think and feel and behave? At the same time, she failed to teach me what I needed to know in order to succeed socially. I now concluded that I could no longer depend upon my mother to successfully guide my life. Neither could I depend upon myself. I floundered, needing someone more capable than my mother to mentor me.

Ego-Neutral replay:

- *Focus on where I was at that moment. Be a polite, interested observer. Make only positive or neutral comments about anything and anyone. The payoff: Less mental stress generated by trying to determine what kind of person other people would like the most, so I could pretend to be that person.*

- *Being "cool" is not an issue. Focus is upon: being polite, neat and clean, reliable (always doing whatever I said I would do).*

- *Participate in some activities that would put me in contact with other people engaged in those same activities and see if friendships evolve from those acquaintances.*

- *Realize that my mother was unable to teach me things that she did not, herself, know. (When that actually happened, years later, I was finally able to stop being angry with her and was able to forgive her.)*

Secondly, that summer I learned to be a waitress. For the first time in my life, this placed me in a group situation in which the members were involved in a common activity and in contact with a lot of people. Since this was an upscale resort, the atmosphere was laid back and congenial. Customers joked with us. I gained confidence dealing with the public. The head waitress served as a nurturing group mother. This place had its pecking order, but one that was far more tolerable than what I had dealt with before. Instead of a judgmental dominator, we had a powerful, but benign, facilitator and I felt like an accepted member of the group. It was a magical summer, and I was very sorry when it ended.

When I returned to school, I obtained part-time work at a local college-oriented café. This probably got me through the remaining three years without dying of loneliness. The owners were an elderly couple who emotionally adopted me. While working in the café, I was able to interact with more students. This reduced my feeling that I should pretend to be someone else. Paradoxically, my grades improved as my outside workload increased. My grades were best when I worked 35 hours per week. With more or fewer hours, the grades became worse. This was probably because work forced me to schedule time to study. Although I was unaware at the time, it was illegal for students to work off campus without permission. The week of my graduation, I was told that the Dean of Women and her friends avoided that café for the three years I worked there so that officially they could not know about me. For that I thank them.

In all of the four years I spent there, I never knew who I was. I was constantly looking to others for cues on how to define myself. I felt no closeness to any other student. When I graduated, it was not with regret for friends and a life I was leaving behind, but with fear for the unknown ahead of me.

To this day, I am haunted by a recurring dream. I am walking across the campus on a dreary, late-autumn day. Students are gathered in small groups, happily talking to each other. I am alone. As I walk past these clusters of students, I hopefully search for a familiar face. No one notices me. No one calls to me. No one even knows my name.

High Life in the Hamptons!

I spent a total of two summers working on Mackinac Island and one summer employed at a resort near Cape Cod. Then I learned there was more money to be had on Long Island, so I obtained a position as the assistant to the owner of a marina and restaurant in East Hampton.

When I arrived, I had lunch at a local restaurant. It was food I don't remember and a gimlet, since alcohol was beginning to be important to me. After all, wasn't the ability to walk into a bar and order a drink a symbol of adulthood? Actually, I felt as isolated and inadequate as I did when I was ten years old. As I sat there, I thought of the anguish I had endured in trying to live up to what I thought were other people's expectations. Then, at that moment, I gave it up. I decided there would be no more pretenses. I would simply do my work and not be concerned about getting people to like me or accept me or approve of me.

Ego-Neutral observation: I almost had it!

- *No more pretenses.*

- *Do my work, focusing on the moment.*

- *Abandon trying to manipulate people into liking me or accepting me or approving of me.*

My employer (alias, Ms. Marina) was a woman approximately the age of my mother. She approved of my work ethic, saw herself in me and wanted to help. She said, "You and I are simpatico, Little One. You don't feel confident now, but by the end of this summer, I will give you a façade that will take you anywhere you want to go. "

Immediately, my Ego-Neutral resolution was discarded. I craved the power in that promise! This was the guidance and source of approval I had needed all of my life! This would elevate me above people who had rejected me in the past and would protect me from being invalidated ever again.

She continued, "You can do it. I did it, and I am an ugly woman. It will be even easier for you since you are beautiful. You didn't know that, did you? If you stand up straight and tell yourself that you belong there, when you walk into a room, every man will turn to look at you." I did those things, and she was right. Every man turned to look at me. Every time. I could hardly believe it! And they did more than just look. They approached me, talked to me, wanted to spend time with me. I'm now sorry to say that it went straight to my head. I, who had been powerless for so long, reveled in this. I could not get enough!

Ego-Neutral replay:

- *Focus on where I was at that moment. Since I was new and the place was unknown to me, first of all, be a polite, interested observer. Make only positive or neutral comments about anything and anyone. The payoff: Less mental stress generated by trying to determine what kind of person these people would like the most, so I could pretend to be that person.*

- *Being desirable, seductive and irresistible is not an issue. Focus is upon: being polite, neat and clean, reliable.*

- *Be interested in what I think of others instead of interested in what others think of me.*

The marina catered to transient yacht traffic, so there was a constant turnover of wealthy customers. The restaurant was small and intimate. There was a family holiday ambience combined with the glamour of money and power. For example, Mayor Wagner from New York City was an occasional guest. I was there all the time, opening the restaurant before noon and working with the owner until closing around 1:00 a.m.

Much of the time, late at night was spent sitting at the bar next to the owner, talking to the customers and drinking. I quickly advanced to three or four drinks per night. Since I weighed only 100 pounds, it hit me pretty hard, but I drank because as long as I was numb I was not so self-conscious. Blurred vision was not uncommon. Every morning began with a hangover, coffee, aspirin and a cigarette. The boss's façade (or my interpretation of it) had not in any way removed my doubts of my adequacy as a human being. Without the alcohol, I was still a shy, needy, awkward person, craving approval and attention.

Ego-Neutral replay:

- *Never drink in order to feel more comfortable with people. Spend time with others without this numbing, alcoholic, emotional crutch.*

- *If sitting at the bar without a drink made me feel uncomfortable, figure out why. Was I bored? If yes, figure out how to be sober and not bored. Maybe spend less time at the bar and go somewhere else to do more interesting things.*

My views about sexual behavior were challenged. My mother had insisted that no decent man would marry a woman who had "done it," so at the age of twenty-one I was still a virgin. Now I learned from my mentor that men did, indeed, marry experienced women. I also learned that it was acceptable to have an occasional social encounter with a married man. My boss introduced me to customers that she felt were appropriate and encouraged me to have dinner with them.

Ego-Neutral replay:

- *Don't depend on others to tell you how to think and feel about such a personal issue.*

- *When in doubt, don't do it.*

- *Be honest.*

- *Stay away from married men. If they will have you, they are cheats and you are a thief, taking something that belongs to someone else.*

Toward the end of the summer, there were days when I had difficulty staying focused on my work. It was easier to drift off into the fantasy of being admired and desired by all men and envied by all women and secure in abundant wealth.

I left for graduate school in September with my virginity still intact, but with a habit of drinking in any possible social situation and guidelines for moral behavior demolished. The only thing I felt I could do was to attempt to emulate my mentor's philosophy and behavior. In short, I was still clueless as to who I was or what I wanted to be. I only knew what I wanted to have – wealth and power.

Later, a psychiatrist would interpret this as rebellion against my mother and the restrictive culture she represented, but it was not rebellion. I simply had to reach out. I had to do something differently, because nothing my mother told me to do seemed to work. I was desperately seeking a workable solution and Ms. Marina's guidelines seemed to promise success and relief.

Can Things Get Any Worse?
Oh, Yes!

After my summer in East Hampton, I arrived in Kansas to enroll in graduate school. I felt as abandoned and lacking in direction as I did my first day at college when my mother walked away from me. My first night away from East Hampton, alone in my rented room, I asked myself, "How will I ever get to sleep tonight without a drink?"

Ego-Neutral replay: Focus on tasks needed to become settled in a new location. Keep thoughts in the present while performing tasks that lead to a better future. Avoid the practice of going to sleep under the influence of alcohol.

Where were the men that had sought my company that summer? Where were the glamour and sense of abundance? Not here. I was now in a dingy office in an ancient building, surrounded by people who believed that college professors made enough money. My colleagues were students who lived from one paycheck to the next. No men turned to look at me when I walked into the room. They were too busy studying.

Ego-Neutral replay: No time wasted on thoughts of glamour, power or manipulating men. Too busy studying and interacting honestly and non-manipulatively with my peers. Focus on being interested instead of interesting.

How should I behave without Ms. Marina to advise me? The only thing she said that seemed to apply in this setting was, "Lose yourself in your work." Unfortunately, the scholastic problems with organization and memory during undergraduate school continued to plague me here. If academic success had been more easily attainable, perhaps the downward spiral of my life would have leveled off. Instead, it accelerated.

What else did she say to do? Oh, yes. "Go to church." I did not do this. Why? For one thing, I did not have a car. The room I rented was within walking distance of the campus. So were the lunch counters and cafeteria where I took my meals. Also, I had not attended church since leaving high school. It had produced no comfort or sense of belonging during those now-distant times, so why bother? Also, it was my prejudgment (based in belief, not fact) that church members in small-town Kansas were bound to be both boring and judgmental and not at all like the powerful, worldly people I had known in East Hampton. I could see no way that church attendance could enhance my life.

Ego-Neutral replay:

- *Focus on where I am at that moment. Since I was new and the place was unknown to me, first of all, be a polite, interested observer. Make only positive or neutral comments about anything and anyone. Put my attention on others, rather than upon what others might be thinking of me.*

- *Do not pre-judge people or groups of people. To decide where a person fits in my life, take each person on a case-by-case basis. Avoid conclusions based on stereotypes or upon another person's perceptions.*

- *Being "accepted" is not an issue. Simply be polite, neat and clean, reliable (always doing whatever I say I will do). This means my attention is not upon trying to get others to like me. On the other hand, I am not doing things that will cause others to dislike me.*

- *Participate in some activities that would put me in contact with other people engaged in those same activities. Then see if friendships evolve from those acquaintances. These activities could be studying with my classmates, playing golf or tennis, going to church, doing volunteer or community service, etc.*

- *Pursue goals or acquire skills that do not depend upon the approval of others in order for me to succeed. For example, doing well in my courses.*

Most of all, I remembered that Ms. Marina said it was OK to have sex before you were married, and it was OK to be involved with married men. This was the most damaging course of action possible. After a few dates with several younger, financially stressed single students, I connected with a local relatively powerful, financially comfortable married man. I was drawn to him because for the moment, at least, his sexual attraction to me made me feel powerful again. I felt that I was very important to this very important man. This was the exciting part of the courtship.

Ego-Neutral replay: No married men. Romantic involvement with a married person other than your own spouse simply pairs a liar and cheat with a thief. No men at all, if the reason for wanting them is to bask in reflected power.

Initially, I was able to pretend that the frustrating part of the courtship was unimportant. That was a big lie to myself in a relationship that was a lie from beginning to end. I could never be seen publicly with this man. I could not talk about him with people I knew. It was also frustrating, because I could not phone him. I had to wait for him to phone me, and I never knew when that would be. I avoided friendships with eligible single men due to some befuddled sense of loyalty to my True Love.

Ego-Neutral replay: With the wrong person in my life, I couldn't even notice the right person if he happened by. Keep obviously wrong people out of my life. This was a wrong person. He was a cheat and a liar. He demonstrated this by violating his marriage vows. What a conceit, to imagine that he would be more honest and faithful with me. Allow into my life only people who at least have potential of being the right person.

81

Over several months, I became increasingly impatient. If he loved me so much and his wife was such a loser, why didn't he divorce her and marry me? I fantasized about how good life would be if he were my husband, and I thought of how empty my life currently was.

At this point, he began to spend less time with me. I would rush home from class so I would be able to answer the phone in case he called. Unable to concentrate on my lessons, I frequently had something to drink. Finally, it would be late enough at night to know that today he would not be calling. I would then fall into a drunken, dreamless sleep. He had a sense of when I had given it up and at that point would touch base just long enough to get me hopeful again. Then, without explanation or warning, he would sever communication.

Ego-Neutral replay: An EN would not have become entrapped in this mess in the first place. At this point, I was addicted to the reluctant lover, feeling horrible without him and almost normal in his presence. He had become a drug. It would have been extremely difficult, but not impossible, to become Ego-Neutral at this point. Dump the emotionally abusive lover – and make it stick! Spend time productively studying with the other students, acquiring comprehension of the material I should have been studying and forming friendships with peers. Relinquish the belief that life can be worth living only if a special someone rescues me.

If street drugs had been readily available, I would probably have added drugs to my excessive use of alcohol. It was my good fortune that this crisis occurred before 1965. My lover brought in marijuana on three separate occasions. That was the extent of my recreational drug use. On one occasion, he brought me some unknown pill. But I already had too much to drink and vomited shortly after taking it. Luck was with me. He had no other pills with him.

Ego-Neutral replay: Don't abuse drugs and alcohol, and don't allow substance abusers into my life. Don't swallow unknown chemicals. Allow people to be important in my life only when they are sufficiently comfortable with themselves that they don't need chemical mind-alterations.

One night I returned from spring break. I thought, surely he would call since I had been gone for so long. Of course, he did not. Restlessly waiting for the phone to ring, I could not sleep. The tension was unbearable. As the night dragged on, I poured another drink and another. Finally, I mentally said, "Why don't I just kill myself?" As the last word ended, I was saturated with the most amazing feeling of tranquility. It was a genuine sense of peace. Perhaps it was because when a person has no future, there is nothing to worry about and nothing more to lose. At any rate, the feeling was so novel that I gratefully experienced it for several hours. As the sun rose, the consuming restlessness and tension returned.

That morning I went to the doctor. Amazingly (to me), the first thing I blurted out was, "I just can't drink anymore!" This was not what I intended to say, but he seemed to think it was important. He set up an appointment for me at the outpatient clinic of the state hospital.

Later that week, I told my tale of woe to a psychiatrist. He asked, "Why are you wasting your time on this married man who isn't going to leave his wife?"

"Because I'm calm when he's with me." Through my tears, the answer I had never before articulated was finally verbalized.

He continued the interview. "Have you ever thought about suicide?"

"Oh, yes," I replied. "I have enough pheno barb to do that."

"Have you ever attempted suicide?"

"No, if I try, I will do a good job of it. Do you think I need therapy?"

He said, "You belong in the hospital!"

I returned to school and spoke to the department head. A medical leave of absence was arranged. I entered the hospital for thirty days of observation, and I remained as a voluntary inpatient for two and a half years.

Sanctuary!

Entering the hospital probably saved my life. I had been on the verge of flunking out of graduate school and had no important significant other to make me feel worthwhile. I saw successful people and knew I was not one of them. I looked in the future and saw a life that was ordinary, with no hope of being better. You might say that I preferred death to mediocrity. Paradoxically, by dying, I could stop being nobody. I would no longer be an outcast. I would no longer be forever unsuccessful in being acceptable and accepted.

From the very beginning, my progress at the hospital was impeded by the issue of trust. I felt betrayed. During my initial outpatient interview, I voiced concern over food. My diet was essentially vegetarian, and I was concerned that I would be required to eat food that I found repugnant. The doctor assured me that patients frequently walked to the fast food place near a corner of the grounds. To my surprise, I was immediately placed on a closed ward and was not allowed to leave the complex for over a month. Before I was admitted, I had expected to be given a one-month intensive treatment and then released. There was a summer job waiting in East Hampton. The staff waited until the end of that month to tell me I would be staying the entire summer. I was very angry that they hadn't told me sooner.

During the first month, I was interviewed by a group of five or six people. At one point, I blurted out, "I have known for a long time that something was wrong." Immediately, I thought I'd better shut up and concentrate on showing them how sane I was. Even though I was voluntary, it was starting to look like they could keep me there for a very long time.

After my physical exam, the psychiatrist met with me. "Before you were admitted here, you said that you were having an affair with a married man. I thought you meant you were physically intimate." I replied, "We were!" Then

85

he asked, "How do you explain the gynecologist's finding that you are still intact?" I exclaimed, "You mean I can still pass as a virgin?" Even as I said that, I realized how defiled I felt and also how dishonest it would be to pretend that nothing had happened. The gynecologist performed another exam and decided that perhaps I was sexually experienced after all. Later that month, I dreamed that objects were pouring out of my vagina: rusted coils, an assortment of dirty sharp-edged metal blades and pieces of broken glass.

After three months, I was moved to an open ward (with a constant grounds-pass) and given two psychotherapy sessions per week. I was also allowed to work off the grounds. I found a part-time job as a research assistant at a local psychiatric foundation. I was given weekend passes. I used them to return to the college town and spend Saturday night with a group of regulars at a local hangout. The resulting hangovers were monumental, aggravated by the quantity of beer and by the Thorazine dispensed by the hospital. Time spent like this was boring, but I felt grateful that these people were willing to let me participate in the group. During that year, I slept with a number of men. I don't even remember their names. Sometimes I did it hoping to be rescued into a better life. Sometimes I did it just to have company for the evening. The encounters were disappointing and completely meaningless. That is what I most regret.

The next one and a half years were spent in a kind of limbo. I was removed from the pressure to sink or swim academically. I wasn't concerned about the people around me liking me. There was still the dream that once I was released I could succeed professionally and be admired by all. I was waiting for therapy to make me perfect. My doctor was waiting for me to say something relevant. It was the classic Mexican standoff.

For example, I asked him what I was supposed to do about dating and sex. After all, neither my mother's advice nor Ms.

Marina's opposing strategy had brought me any satisfaction, relief or sense of direction. He replied to my question with the detached observation, "You seem to want other people to tell you what to do." I was annoyed by the response. Of course! I had just *asked* him what to do! His reply made my question appear trivial.

In retrospect, he was trying to guide the session into a more productive line of thought. I was focused on having an authority answer my questions. He was trying to get me to understand that I needed to be my own authority. Unfortunately, he didn't say that. At that point, I wish he could have given me the book you are reading at this moment. If he had done so, and stated (with authority) that this is what it was all about, I could have moved forward with my life. My focus should not have been, "Should I or shouldn't I?" My question should have been, *How do I really feel about this?*

Walking to a session one day, I thought that maybe I should talk about wanting people to like me. I was deeply embarrassed even to admit that I was not likable, but *needing* to be liked. It was near the end of the session before I broached the subject. Instead of encouraging me to continue the topic in our next session, the frustrated doctor responded, "I have to wonder why you waited until the end of the hour to bring this up." Taking this as a rebuke, I did not mention it again for over a year.

As I remained in the hospital, time passed. I felt a satisfying future seeping away. Then one day in mid-spring, the doctor dropped the bombshell. His residency was ending, and he was leaving. Within less than two months, he would be gone. "Of course," he said, "I will recommend more therapy." I realized that tears were running down my face. I was abandoned once again. Now there wasn't even a hope or dream of a better life. In two months, I would again have no future worth wanting.

Don't Try This at Home!

I left the session, frantic to accomplish in two months what had not been achieved in one and a half years. I started free-associating on my own. Starting with one unhappy event, I would recall a prior comparable event, and so on. This brought no new insight but increased distress over the hopelessness of my current situation. Then one night, I dreamed that I was overwhelmed with panic in response to an unseen, unknown source. As I watched, the hair of my dream-self changed from black to white. When I awoke, the terror was still present! It remained with me every waking moment for several years.

I had not received tranquilizers in over a year. When I approached the ward doctor to get something, his reply was, "If you have problems, work it out in therapy."

I cannot even begin to describe the intensity of what I felt. It was complete and endless terror in every particle of my being. But there was nothing to run from and no place to hide! There was no threat to escape or conquer so that the fear would subside. I felt that if I became any more afraid I would no longer know who or what I was and would forever lose my ability to know the world around me. Not only was I terrified. I was terrified of being even more terrified. It felt as if a rupture had occurred. I was standing on a trapdoor that opened into Hell and any moment it would snap down and dump me into eternal mindless horror. At other times, I felt like my inner soul was a volcano, jarring my hold on sanity at the slightest emotional provocation, threatening to bury me in orange glowing lava.

It was relentless. I felt like this **all of the time**! I washed windows or scrubbed the floor in an attempt to focus on the moment and to ignore the panic. Earlier in my stay at the hospital, I had read a book entitled *I Never Promised You a*

Rose Garden. Now, I frantically attempted NOT to think about it. I was obsessed with the notion that reading it would trigger some stray thought that would escalate the terror. I avoided reading the word "Freud" for the same reason. I tried desperately not to think of my past, except in the presence of the psychiatrist. With two more months of the only treatment option left for me, I returned to my session. I can't even remember what I said. I only recall that I cried throughout each meeting. However, I found that I was able to talk through the tears. The tears were from tension and had no apparent relationship to what was being said.

Nearly two years into therapy, I finally addressed the one and only problem that had so completely poisoned my life and had a stunning realization. I was crying and telling the doctor, "You know, there IS no way I can make people like me. *THERE IS NOTHING I CAN DO TO MAKE PEOPLE LIKE ME!* The *only thing* I can do is be neat and clean and polite and see if they will tolerate my presence."

I noticed the doctor was nodding his head. Emphatically! Then the thought formed. *THIS IS REALLY TRUE! I HAD NEVER KNOWN THIS WAS TRUE! WHY HAD NO ONE TOLD ME?* All that needless anguish! All those countless moments of unhappiness! For more than half of my life, I had been immersed in a contest that no one can ever truly win. *Every waking moment, for fifteen years, I had been playing a fool's game!*

This was the first positive turning point in my life since I was seven years old! When I walked out of his office that day, I didn't have this book to guide me. I didn't know exactly what I was going to do, except that I would not play that game anymore. I was going to be honest with myself. I would no longer ask, "What *should* I be thinking?" Instead, I would ask, "What *do I* think?" I would not ask, "What *should* I be feeling (so I can be like important others)?" but "What *do I* feel?" Instead of compulsively seeking opportunities to make others like me or to make myself feel more important than others, I would focus on attaining worthwhile goals. In this case, the choice of goal was easy. I would return to the school situation that I had fled from two years earlier, at the age of twenty-three. This time, learning for the sake of learning would give purpose to my life.

I attained more honesty and empowerment that day than I had experienced in the entire fifteen preceding years.

Transformation to Ego-Neutral

This is how I became Ego-Neutral. I realized that even though my focus had changed, there would be people who just would not like me, for whatever reason. Probably that reason would have nothing to do with how I had treated them. I knew it would make me uncomfortable and there would be little that I could deliberately do to change it.

What would I do if this happened? I asked myself, "What is the worst thing that can happen if someone doesn't like me? Can they cut off my head?" The answer to that was, "No. They cannot cut off my head. Not at this time and place."

Since death was not going to occur as a result of being disliked, I decided that whatever happened, I would continue behaving as I was before I discovered the negative judgment. *I would not give any abusively judgmental person the power to change my focus, my activity or my feelings about myself.* That meant that I would not allow my attention to be derailed by hating them for not liking me. I would not reflexively retaliate. I would civilly keep the lines of communication open. This means that I would do nothing rude to that person in return. If I had actually done something wrong, I would take responsibility for it and apologize. If I was unaware of having been rude, I would ask if I had done something to offend them. As long as there was a possible exchange of ideas between us, there was also the chance that the source of the attacker's upset could be known and addressed. Possibly a misunderstanding could be resolved. If communication were severed, the entire negative circumstance would freeze for both of us and never change.

In an effort to channel my thoughts away from the ongoing panic, I resumed studying and discovered that I could both understand and remember the subject matter. When my therapist left, I announced that I wanted to return to graduate school. Finally, at last, they were willing to release me. I followed the steps that were outlined in the section of this book entitled *What To Do and Why*.

I became aware of my motives and emotions, striving for this focus to become second nature. If anything made me feel uncomfortable, I would ask, "Why am I feeling this way?" Then I would try to answer the question.

For example, discomfort from reading a textbook typically arose because I didn't fully understand what was being discussed. I then would re-read things earlier in the chapter as well as further studying the point of uneasiness. If necessary, I would ask other classmates about their understanding. Finally, as I came to fully understand the topic, the sense of unease would vanish.

If an encounter with another person left me feeling uncomfortable, I also would ask, "Why am I feeling this way?" There was no simple answer to this, since no two encounters are the same. Sometimes, I addressed the matter as it happened. I could do this by saying to the other person, "I'm not sure I understand." Other times, while I knew what had caused the discomfort, I might be confused on how to respond. Rather than say something that might create a complete break in communication, I would examine the situation later and determine what, if anything, to do or what could have been safely done.

I was neat and clean. I did this first thing in the morning and then focused on other matters. To avoid calling attention to myself, I dressed conservatively.

When I was with others, I focused on them instead of myself. If I had a question, my focus was on the question instead of myself. I talked to men person to person, rather than flirty young female to desirable male. My conversations were to exchange knowledge, not to emotionally manipulate others.

I attempted to be reliable, civil and honest. I learned that I could do all of these things, despite feeling absolutely horrible.

When I realized that I didn't understand something, I was able to ask for clarification, rather than pretending that I understood it.

I embarked on a path of self-improvement, which required skill, rather than approval of others, to attain success. This was done when I resumed graduate work. An added bonus was that being deeply involved in study kept me sane by giving me some distraction from the constantly present panic. My test scores were outstanding. Along with the ongoing fear, I also experienced a deeply gratifying sense of accomplishment.

I became involved in activities that increased my contact with people. I focused on participating in the activity, rather than in trying to gain favor with the other participants. For the most part, this was accomplished by studying with and taking coffee breaks with my classmates. Also, I joined the Graduate Student Bowling League to increase my contact with people outside of my academic area.

I discovered that I was basically not a joyful person. At the time, I was not thinking in terms of genetic predisposition or brain chemistry. I simply recognized this about me, and I accepted it. If I was not happy, at least I was no longer desperately unhappy. Without question, my life had substantially improved. If I could not be happy, I could, instead, be curious and active in satisfying that curiosity. From the day we are born, all of us are passing time until we die. I was determined to find this interlude interesting and to fill it with constructive goal-oriented actions.

Initially, I stopped using alcohol in order to confront social situations with my feelings undistorted. To my surprise, I felt all right for having abstained. Never in my life had I felt happier after taking a drink, so the only thing being abandoned was a fraudulent sense of belonging.

Several months before my psychiatrist announced his coming departure, I had successfully stopped smoking. Later, despite the emotional stress, the stress from academic pressures and the stress of interacting with others in a way entirely new to me, I did not resume smoking. In part, I did this by using competing responses. Sitting with others at a table during coffee break, for example, I would shred a paper napkin. When restlessness that previously would have triggered smoking occurred, I would look at the restlessness and ask myself, "Will smoking really make this go away for longer than it takes to finish a cigarette?" The answer was, "No." If I were trying to put off doing something I did not want to do, I would ask, "Can I procrastinate without smoking?" Or maybe I would just do the unpleasant task. Then there was nothing to delay. Sometimes I would negotiate with myself. "If I still feel this way **tomorrow**, *MAYBE* I'll have a cigarette *then*. But *NOT* today!" In this way, I never stopped smoking forever. I never stopped smoking for longer than twenty-four hours. When tomorrow became today, I repeated the exercise and the decision.

I also ended casual, indifferent, sexual behavior. It had not made me happy and had routinely left me feeling depressed and used. Given this downside and the absence of any benefit, continuing the old pattern would have been *really stupid*, lacking in self-honesty and self-defeating. I no longer succumbed simply in order to avoid spending an evening alone. I no longer searched for someone to rescue me from a disappointing life. I was able to be unattached without feeling incomplete. Oh, yes! And no more married men! Taking a married lover is not Ego-Neutral behavior. That is stealing and an Ego-Neutral person seeks only fair exchange.

First Year on My Own

This chapter is called *First Year on My Own* because it was the first year that I looked only to myself for answers. There was no mentor, no confidant, nor an all-knowing person to dispense the correct answer for each issue I had to address. Nor did I want such advice. I now realized that answers needed to come from me, even if they produced less-than-perfect results.

I also returned to graduate school facing the strong possibility that I might not academically succeed. I had decided to give it my very best effort anyway. If I then failed, it was a clear sign that this was not the path in life that I should take – that something better suited to me should be discovered and pursued. If I failed, it would not be the end of the world, nor would I be branded a failure in my own eyes. The only true failure would be failing to try.

I remained in the hospital until fall classes began. The day before I was to enroll in graduate school, my father killed himself. I had been studying an application of the Guttman Scale. It attempted to define a fixed order of physiological responses to emotional stress. Accordingly, when a threat arises, first there is an increase in heart rate and the mouth goes dry. If the stress becomes more severe, then, in addition to elevated pulse and dry mouth, there is tightening of the stomach followed by the need for a bowel movement. At the highest stress level, an intense need to urinate is added to the preceding conditions. These responses reliably occur in this order.

Unexpectedly, I was told to phone my father's house. Immediately my pulse shot up and mouth went dry. What could be wrong? Everything had seemed so normal. And right now, I needed everything to be normal! As I placed the call, my stomach began to churn. Someone on the other end said, "Well, you've lost your father." At that moment, I needed to have a bowel movement in the worse way. I had perfectly progressed through this Guttman Scale.

The unthinkable had happened. Weren't parents supposed to be there forever? Of course, he had been in a downward spiral for years. I knew that. Much of each day was spent drinking coffee and smoking one cigarette after another. The remainder of each day was spent drinking alcohol and smoking one cigarette after another. It was a life devoid of goals and purpose and hope. The upside was he had remarried someone who could afford to supply him with plenty of coffee, cigarettes and alcohol. Finally, he had had enough. I understood that he could be so unhappy that death would be a welcome release. I had been there myself. This knowledge did not lessen the pain of knowing he was gone forever and would never have the chance to get better.

The hospital staff told me not to attend the funeral. They also prescribed Equanil, describing it as a very mild tranquilizer. I was reluctant to take it, fearing that it would depress my ability to hold the ever-present panic at bay. Finally, I agreed to take it, and the next day I enrolled in graduate school. There was no change in the level of terror. I had a number of crying spells, of course. As I've written this chapter, thirty-eight years later, several times my throat has tightened and tears have not been far away.

I focused on getting through each moment as it arrived in my existence. I became deeply involved in my studies. This kept my attention off the constant panic and also reduced the time I spent grieving. To my surprise and delight, my understanding and retention were outstanding, and this was reflected in my test scores. I had decided that each time I made an 'A' on a test I would reward myself by purchasing new clothes. That plan didn't last long. I was making too many outstanding grades to afford it.

My ability to grasp class material was deeply gratifying. I related each topic to my life. The subject didn't matter. I did this with sensory processes, social psychology, learning theory and statistics. The latter was a subject I had nearly flunked before taking an incomplete and entering the hospital. The statistics professor approached me, and said, "Usually people outside of the statistics department don't do that well in this course. I assumed you were taking it because it was a requirement and you just needed it to get by. But you are one of the top students in the class. I just wanted you to know that you are doing outstanding work."

There were other indications that I was on the right path. I came across someone I had known from the pre-hospital days. He attempted to communicate to me from that perspective. Very quickly, he said, "You have changed." Later, he said it again. Another male student said, "At my undergraduate school, we listed the traits of an ideal female. You are like that person." These remarks did not make me feel big and important and pleased with myself, as they would have a year earlier. They did, however, confirm that by my following some simple principles, other people might see me as an acceptable and even desirable member of the human race. I no longer felt like an outcast. I also recognized that how others perceived me had become a non-issue for me. I did not need their good opinions to feel all right about myself. By the same token, their negative opinions had no impact on my self-image. In fact, I was unconcerned about feeling either good or bad about myself. Instead, my focus was upon using each current moment in the most beneficial and constructive way possible.

At the end of the first semester, I returned to the hospital to report in and to get my prescription renewed. There was a new ward doctor who decided I didn't need Equanil any longer. I asked him to wean me off of it, but he said that wasn't necessary. I should just stop taking it. I was very concerned that ending medication would cause the panic to escalate. To my relief, this did not happen.

Shortly into the new semester, I noticed that if I didn't have a date for the approaching weekend, sometime during Friday, I would experience an increasingly intense feeling of dread. This would disperse when classes resumed on Monday. As time passed, the dread began on Thursday and then Wednesday! If this continued, it would impact me all the time. It was like a lead weight pressing on me. I could barely get out of bed on those days. Fortunately, the dread did not overwhelm the never-ending panic, and it was this panic that drove me out of bed and into the classroom so that I could continue ignoring it. It is difficult to imagine that two such unpleasant, overwhelming emotional states could exist at the same time. Trust me. They can.

In retrospect, I might have been able to deal successfully with this condition by spending my dateless weekend evenings at my pre-hospital hangout. To revisit that scene while thoroughly grounded in an Ego-Neutral mode might have held the depression at bay. I could have safely engaged in the competing response of talking to people instead of being alone in my office. That might have been enough to get me through the weekend. Why didn't I do this? That option did not occur to me until thirty-eight years later – when I wrote this chapter. My Ego-Neutral focus was so far removed from my old life, I simply did not think of returning to any of it.

Depression seems like such an inadequate word to describe this overwhelming feeling. It continued for several weeks. Why didn't I go back to the hospital? Because the only help they had extended for unbearable terror had been talk therapy. I saw no way I could talk away this enormous weight on my existence. It didn't even occur to me that the hospital had anything that could help. Three years would pass before I realized that I had undergone an unrecognized, unsupervised drug withdrawal. If I had been weaned, as I requested, it is possible the depression would not have occurred.

So, how did the depression end? I soon met my husband-to-be. Suddenly, there were no more dateless weekends. Was this the reason the depression lifted? Or was relief due to biochemical aspects of romantic involvement? I was completely besotted and immersed in romance and physical attraction. It was a classic case of hormones run amuck! I couldn't touch him enough. I couldn't get close enough to him. While ongoing panic remained, overwhelming depression vanished. Was it the change in body chemistry that made me better? I can only speculate. How did this differ from previous romantic involvement? Simply this: I did not need him in order to approve of myself. Four weeks into dating, I told him about my time in the hospital. If it was going to be an issue for him, I wanted it on the table then. If he wanted out, I would be unhappy, but I would understand. Two weeks later, he proposed, and four months after that we were married.

One month before the wedding, I began taking birth control pills. I still clearly recall that evening. Sitting on the edge of my bed, while holding a glass of water in one hand and the first pill in the other hand, I reviewed the events of the past year. Throughout courtship, I still successfully continued a heavy academic schedule. During spring semester, I had successfully completed the requirements to enter the Ph.D. program. I had completed my thesis and all requirements for the M.S. degree. Despite the ongoing panic, I was functioning at a truly gratifying level of ability and accomplishment. Briefly, I thought that I should not marry until panic had finally subsided. Then I decided to proceed. Ongoing terror might be with me forever. Even with it, I could still have a good life, sharing it with someone I loved.

Obviously being Ego-Neutral made my life with constant panic better than it would have been with constant panic *plus* Ego-Defense. It *also* made my life **better than it was *in any prior panic-free time*.** It was better than pre-hospital graduate school, in undergraduate school, and better than in high school and grade school. There were now people with whom I could communicate freely on a variety of subjects. There were people with whom I could share my thoughts and feelings without anxiety over what they would think of me. My concern over what others felt toward me was enormously reduced. My academic performance was deeply gratifying. My professional future was highly promising.

In anticipation and celebration, as though it were a sacrament, I swallowed the first contraceptive pill and entered a new life. Unfortunately, the light at the end of the tunnel was indeed from an oncoming train! That, however, is the subject for a book that may be written if this book generates enough income for me to retire from my current job. I will only say, that without an Ego-Neutral orientation, I could not have survived the coming challenges.

In Conclusion

It may be helpful at this point to read the how-to part of this book and review some of your own life, doing Ego-Neutral replays. If you don't know where to start, begin with yesterday. When and how could you have been Ego-Neutral yesterday? Then review the day before yesterday. And so on. As you move through your life in reverse, turning points (both good and bad) in your life will become apparent. Were you Ego-Neutral at those times? How could you have used those times to better advantage if you had been Ego-Neutral?

A full-life review is not essential in order for you to transcend the pecking order. You do not have to go all the way back to an unhappy childhood or an ugly adolescence. Everything is actually done now, in present time. It should, however, be very useful to review the way you relate to people you are currently seeing frequently. Is your relationship with them Ego-Defensive? How can you be Ego-Neutral with these same people?

It was necessary for me to sink to enormous depths of hopelessness and personal corruption in order to *discover* the concepts and principles that ultimately restored my life. It is *not* necessary for *you* to hit bottom in order to *apply* these principles to your own life and experience positive personal transformation. You can improve your life this very day.

This autobiography reveals how the Ego-Neutral approach to life could have been applied to my situations, beginning at the age of ten. We will never know where my life would have gone, had I become Ego-Neutral at an earlier age. Certainly, it would have been less stressful because I would not have been constantly judging myself. We can only observe the downward spiral and loss of self and self-esteem that actually unfolded because I was *not* Ego-Neutral.

In retrospect, I could have had a truly satisfying life during those fifteen years. They were, instead, dismal and hopeless. All of the things I craved, all of the things I needed, all of the things that would have made my life better had been there for me all the time. All I had to do was apply Ego-Neutral principles to recognize the satisfying friendships, relationships, activities and accomplishments that were already there.

For example, during college, I constantly felt the need for some well-adjusted, successful, powerful man to rescue me. Then everything would be all right. I spent much unproductive time daydreaming, sleeping and avoiding people. Had I been Ego-Neutral, I would have immersed myself in my studies and possibly found a study partner for some of my courses. Better academic performance would have vastly improved my future career opportunities and income. Also, I would have spent more time in the library with the intention of actually learning something. A side benefit **might** have been that other people would have known of my existence and known me in an Ego-Neutral mode. In this setting, I **might** have actually met the ideal mate and been able to recognize him as the ideal person for me. This same person could not have met my distorted, Ego-Defensive needs at all and would have escaped my notice.

The problem was that I could not see through the Ego-Defensive haze that surrounded me. The opportunities were there, but I was unable to recognize them. This blindness arose from the Ego-Defensive pecking-order tendency that is in all of us when we are born.

Being Ego-Neutral is not simply an alternative way to view the world and yourself. It is the *only* way that you have a chance to gain genuine, enduring satisfaction. Being Ego-Neutral enables you to recognize and experience what is truly important to human existence. Also, being Ego-Neutral allows you to be satisfied because you are now able to know and feel when you actually have enough.

It could well be that many of the things you need for a truly satisfying life are there for you right now. However, their attainability and ability to satisfy you may be distorted by your ego. Being Ego-Neutral is, in an objective way, to fully participate in constructive activities and in the current moment. Share events with others, rather than using events and others to further an agenda of self-aggrandizement. Then see what destiny brings the Ego-Neutral, optimal you.

I can already hear the excuses to avoid following the program:

This is too simple!
Why should I believe this will make my life better?

You should **NOT** BELIEVE it!

✓ You should accept it as a working hypothesis.
✓ Then act on it to **see for yourself** if your life gets better!
✓ At that point, it may become, for you, a fact.

You cannot with certainty conclude that the program works or does NOT work until you have personally tested it.

There are too many things to do!

No, there are only a few things to do.

✓ **ALWAYS** Be Honest With Yourself and strive to be honest with others.
✓ Be Reliable (do what you said you would do when you said you would do it).
✓ Be Polite.
✓ Be Clean and Neat in Appearance.
✓ Don't be a show-off.

- ✓ Embark on self-improvement goals that require skill, rather than the approval of others, in order for you to succeed. Constructive, goal-oriented focus is *essential* for a satisfying life.

- ✓ Expand your opportunities for sharing activities with a wider variety of people. This can be combined with the previous step.

- ✓ Use competing responses in situations that make you feel uncomfortable or self-conscious. *When you are intensely focused on performing a task or gaining information, you cannot at the same time engage in Ego-Defensive perceptions, emotions and addictive behaviors.*

- ✓ Daily, remind yourself that it is **impossible** for you to *make* people like and respect you. However, you *can* keep the door open for people to enter your life and for you to be invited by others into their lives. You can accomplish this by avoiding behaviors that drive others away. Adhere to the above guidelines and transform your Ego-Defensive issues into an Ego-Neutral strategy of interfacing with the world.

THAT'S IT!

The catch is, you must actually *do* these things in order to make your life better.

Just reading this book and agreeing with it will not change anything.

Just reading this book and disagreeing with it is also a futile exercise. *You are in no position to say it won't work until you have thoroughly and consistently practiced the above.*

You can do it today!

I wish you well!

CONTACT THE AUTHOR
www.egoneutral.com

APPENDIX

Appendix A

Classic Ego-Defensive Victor

Recently, I took a plane to the coast. Lucky me! I got to sit in the middle seat! A male, high school student, absorbed in a magazine, sat by the window. Thank goodness! Then the passenger on the aisle arrived, introduced himself in a confident manner and shook my hand. He was approximately college age and determined to talk. Reluctantly, I put my book away. This is some of the conversation that transpired. I have changed names and tweaked descriptions to disguise the involved party. His alias for this book is "Alan."

Early in the flight we hit a little turbulence.

Alan: I wonder why the air gets bumpy.

Me: It happens more often in summer than winter. This is because as surface air gets warm it rises, displacing higher colder air. It's like the wind blowing, only up-and-down instead of sideways.

Alan: What do you think about Kobe Bryant?

Me: I haven't been interested in it. I don't think we will ever really know what happened.

Alan: I don't give a damn about rain forests. They can destroy all of them as far as I'm concerned. (Then he looked at me intently, possibly hoping for a reaction.)

Me: I haven't given it a lot of thought, but it is my understanding that rain forests are a major source of oxygen for the planet. I hate to think what things would be like without them.

Alan: Oh. I didn't think of that.

Alan: Do the employees on the airline seem older to you? I usually fly Southwest, and they seem a lot younger than these people are.

Me: You are not imagining it. This is American Airlines and recently they barely avoided going into Chapter 11. The people who still have jobs are the ones with the most seniority. Of course, upper management behaved badly. Initially, they protected their own compensation and pension fund while throwing the employees to the wolves.

Alan: Oh, No! That's exactly what the executives should do! They should take everything from the company that they can!

Me: Do you have any more questions?

Alan: No.

Me: Why don't you tell me about the turning points in your life?

Alan: Well, my mother was a trophy wife. Then my father found someone younger, but I didn't know about it. After I left home to go to college, they got divorced! They planned it before I left and *didn't even tell me!* When I found out, I was furious with everyone and everything. In a rage all the time! At football practice, I hurt everyone I could. When the coach called me over, I just threw my helmet on the ground and walked away. I never went back. Within a few months, my favorite uncle and two friends died. Then I started drinking a lot and doing drugs: Cocaine, Crystal Meth and Ecstasy.

Ego-Neutral replay: Following the divorce and the deaths of important people, he could have focused on doing well in sports and doing well in his courses and making new friends instead of indulging in drugs and self-pity. EN would have focused anger on the parents, not on innocent bystanders.

Finally, I met a girl I really, really liked. She got me to stop using drugs. We dated for about a year, and I decided to propose. I had it all planned. I even bought the ring. We were going to take a trip to a special place. Then I would bring out the ring. Only before I could do it, she dumped me! The guys I used to hang out with are really happy I'm back! They didn't like her at all. They thought she had ruined me. I'm really a bad boy now. When I was dating her I was (here he hesitated, groping for the precise word)...

Me: Model Citizen?

Alan: Yes, a Model Citizen. But now, I'm back to full-fledged bad boy!

Ego-Neutral replay: Following the end of the relationship, he continues being a Model Citizen because he truly had changed to EN. He realizes that chances of meeting another satisfactory companion for life are reasonably good. He does not return to previous substance abuse and ED companions.

At this point the passenger sitting by the window passed his magazine to Alan, and they started talking about trucks. Alan described one he recently owned. Thumbing through the magazine, he found a picture of the model. "That's it! That's my truck!"

Me: What happened to your truck?

Alan: I was in a wreck, and it got totaled.

Me: How did that happen?

Alan: I was DWI and lost control.

Me: Was anyone hurt?

Alan: The girl in the other car got a broken arm. But I don't care about that bitch!

Me (startled): Why not?

Alan: She sued me for a million dollars, just for a lousy broken arm! F**k her!

Me: Why are *you* angry? You invaded her life in a very violent way, and it sounds like it was entirely avoidable!

Alan: I don't care what happens to her! F**k her! F**k her! F**k her! F**k her!

Shortly after that, the plane landed.

Ego-Neutral replay: Doesn't drink to excess. Doesn't drive when drinking. In a wreck, honestly reviews and accepts his own culpability in the matter instead of blaming everything on the actual victim.

Now you have been introduced to Alan. Is he Little Boy Lost or Monster in the Making? Certainly he is hurt and clueless – and dangerous and uncaring and totally lacking in a sense of responsibility. Throughout his narratives, he presented himself as the sole victim. His conclusion: Being a victim relieves him of any responsibility for his selfish irresponsible behavior. He seems to believe that destructive behavior without consequence is a sign of strength and that winning is everything. He is a classic Ego-Defensive Victor.

Appendix B

Comparison

Ego-Defensive	Ego-Neutral
Driven by belief	Guided by observation
Winner-take-all	Win-Win
Failure	Learning experience
Dominate	Facilitate or remain uninvolved
Abusive	Supportive or Neutral
Manipulative	Forthright
Selective awareness of facts	Awareness of all available facts
Fixes blame	Fixes problem
Blames others for his failures	Accountable for his failures
Takes full credit for success	Gives credit where credit is due
Exclusive	Inclusive
Insatiable	Recognizes and enjoys enough
Competes with others	Improves self with no reference to others

Ego-Defensive	Ego-Neutral
Habitually judges others	Discretely judges others
Deeply upset when rejected	Objective when rejected
Subjective	Objective
Prima donna	Team player
Steals	Exchanges
Feels better about self	Feels better
Goals involve self-image	Goals involve non-self-image interests
Strives for recognition	Strives for accomplishment
May use destruction in order to gain recognition	Will use creation in order to achieve a goal
Enjoys fooling others	Honest in relating to others

Appendix C

Ego-Defensive (ED) vs. Neutral (EN) Examples

Scenario 1: Good deed

While driving down a highway, a person sees an elderly lady pulled off the road with a flat tire. He interrupts his journey to change the tire for her.

ED Behavior: The ED will make sure that other people know about his good deed. ED will make a point of relating the incident in detail to numerous people, whether or not it is easily introduced into the conversation. His goal is to impress as many people as possible with what a generous, admirable person he is. In this way, he feels he has elevated his position in the viewpoint of others.

EN Behavior: He mentions the incident to no one. This is because his entire focus of the incident was to insure that help that was needed and wanted was actually provided. Only if someone asks why he is late in arriving, or how he got dirt on his clothes, will he relate what happened and that is done with very little detail about himself. He is not attempting to impress the listener with what a generous, admirable person he is. He is not attempting to manipulate his position in the viewpoint of others.

Scenario 2: Gift giving

A friend's birthday is approaching.

ED Behavior: ED gives something that he assumes the recipient will like. Then he tells other people how generous he has been. He is very concerned that the recipient adequately appreciates what he has done. If the recipient's response is lukewarm, this is taken as a personal insult. The giver has given the gift, but with the implicit stipulation that the recipient be enthusiastically grateful. ED has used the giving as a means to try to make others think well of him and to feel good about himself. This is an attempt to improve his pecking-order position in the viewpoint of others.

EN Behavior: EN tries to find out what the recipient likes. He may learn this by asking friends or observing the recipient or by asking the recipient what he enjoys. EN gives the gift. He knows it has been received. The focus is on providing what the recipient wants or likes rather than being concerned that the recipient adequately appreciates what the EN has done. If the recipient's response is lukewarm, it is no big deal. EN has given the gift with no strings attached and that includes the string of gratitude. He mentions the gift to others only if asked a direct question, e.g., "So what did you get Judy for her birthday?"

Scenario 3: Talking about other people

ED Behavior: The Ego-Defensive person thrives on gossip. He delights in passing on to as many people as possible anything that makes the subject of the gossip appear inadequate in some way. By contrast, the gossiping person can then feel more adequate. Also, by passing on embarrassing news about someone else, the gossiping person can feel he is more knowledgeable than the person to whom he is talking. So he manages to score two big points at someone else's expense.

EN Behavior: The Ego-Neutral person does not gossip. When EN talks about others, it is in a factual or approving way. EN does *not* delight in delivering embarrassing news about someone else. He does not gossip in an attempt to appear knowledgeable.

Scenario 4

A group of people starts laughing as you enter the room.

ED Behavior: ED automatically assumes that they are laughing at him. ED assumes the other people see him as much lower in the pecking order than they are. He either gets angry with the people who are laughing or deeply embarrassed and overwhelmed with feelings of inadequacy and shame.

EN Behavior: EN walks up to the group and asks, "What's so funny? I want to laugh, too." Immediate response to the laughter is curiosity with no self-consciousness (he has no self-consciousness).

Scenario 5

Someone screams at you: "YOU SON-OF-A-BITCH!"

ED Response: JACKASS!

EN Response: Why did you say that?

EN Searches for all facts. Tries to determine if or how he has upset person #1. If there is a misunderstanding, he will attempt to clear it up. If he has caused someone loss, he will apologize and try to make it right. If he is being unfairly attacked, he will take steps to neutralize this influence. If nothing else works, he counterattacks. ED behavior is never his **first** *response.*

Scenario 6

Person #1: Ever since I let you into my life, you have done nothing but push me away. You obviously aren't interested in a romantic relationship, so I'm going back to Joe.

Person #2: You are so neurotic and possessive!

ED Response:

Person #1: And you are a manipulative, abusive jerk!

Instead of focusing on desired result, which, in this case, is the end of the relationship with person #2, ED Person #1 is immediately drawn into a duel of insults which neither party will really be able to win. Rage escalates.

EN Response:

Person #1: I'm not interested in exchanging insults. All I want is out.

EN focuses on desired result, which, in this case, is the end of the relationship with person #2. Sticks to the facts and refuses to be drawn into an ED duel of insults.

Scenario 7

Cindy has her hair styled.

ED: Cindy has a new haircut and now she really thinks she's cute!

ED looks for negative points in others and communicates disapproval whenever possible. The non-verbalized hope is that in making others less, the ED will somehow look better by contrast.

EN: Doesn't Cindy's new haircut look nice?

EN looks for good points in others and communicates approval when it can honestly be done.

Scenario 8

Person #1: Jim just got accepted into Harvard Business School.

ED: Mr. Big Shot is going to double his hat size now.

ED tries to turn the wins of others into losses. The non-verbalized hope is that in making others less, the ED will somehow look better by contrast.

EN: Good for him!

EN is supportive of the wins of others.

Scenario 9

Person # 1: I just found out that my academic rank is eighth in a class of 100! That means I'll probably get into the college of my choice.

Other person: Did you hear that Susan ranks fourth in our class?

ED Response (Person #1): That's just because she studies all the time. If she was in all the activities that I'm in, her rank wouldn't be that high!

ED attacks someone she perceives has outperformed her. Attempts to diminish the accomplishment of the other person and thereby to appear smarter than the other person.

EN Response (Person #1): Good for her!

EN calmly acknowledges the accomplishment of another. Considers the other person a fellow traveler in life, rather than an opponent to be attacked.

Scenario 10

ED: If you can get your hands out of your pockets, would you get over here and help me?

ED confirms his superior position in the pecking order by insulting a subordinate and then requiring the subordinate to provide help.

EN: If you can spare a little time, would you please help me?

EN treats as an equal the person he hopes will help him. Help from the other person is viewed as a favor, not entitlement.

Scenario 11

(New boss to longtime employee): Why are you doing this task this way?

Employee: That's the way I was trained. I guess that's the way we've always done it.

ED (New Boss): You know, there are dozens of unemployed people out there who would be happy to do it <u>my</u> way.

Note: This is the first time ED has even mentioned a preferred way to perform the task. The pretended goal of the ED is to improve performance of the task. ED's real and hidden goal is to frighten the employee and to make the employee feel helpless. ED has deliberately twisted the employee's answer to a direct question into a statement of defiance.

EN (New Boss): I'd like to try another way. I think this will improve your productivity. Let's see.

EN focuses on improving productivity instead of intimidating the employee. EN establishes a judgement-free environment in which the employee becomes a partner in improving work performance. It is a win-win situation.

Scenario 12

Daughter: (Crying) I'm pregnant, and I don't know what to do!

ED Parent: Oh, no! How could you do this to me? What will my friends think?

ED parent's primary focus is on what other people may think about the parent. Reaction is entirely self-centered.

EN Parent: Calm down! Don't cry! I'm glad you were able to tell me. We'll get through this somehow.

EN parent focuses on daughter's predicament and feelings, rather than upon her own thoughts and feelings.

Scenario 13

Person #1: Ann, do you remember that sweater I loaned you? It's been a while and I would like to wear it next week.

ED (Ann): I hate to tell you this, but the dog ate it. I was really upset because you said it was expensive. I'm really sorry.

Person # 1: Well, aren't you going to replace it?

ED: No. I told you. It's not my fault. The dog ate it. But I'm really sorry. I've noticed that you have been looking really tired and sad lately. I hate to see that. I want to see you with a happy face!

ED refuses to repair any damage she has caused to another person or that person's property. Then ED attempts to make the injured party think that the ED is really concerned about her welfare.

EN (Ann): I hate to tell you this, but the dog ate it. I was really upset because you said it was expensive. I should have told you sooner, but I've been shopping everywhere trying to replace it. No one seems to have that style anymore. I know it's not the same thing, but if you'll pick out another sweater, I'll be happy to pay for it.

EN attempts to repair any damage she has caused to another person or that person's property. She is unwilling for others to pay for her carelessness. She is willing to be accountable.

Scenario 14

An angry, divorced man.

ED: I'm going to drop my kids' health insurance. That'll fix my ex.

ED goes for domination and revenge. Uses shotgun approach that can injure innocent bystanders. In this case, the child is the innocent bystander. ED puts his own satisfaction above the safety of others.

EN: I hope my ex and I can work through things without hurting the kids.

EN works with situation, strives for cooperation, doesn't seek revenge, doesn't shotgun-blast the wrong target.

Scenario 15

Person # 1: I never go to movies by myself.

ED hears this and thinks, "I go to movies by myself a lot. I guess I can't do that anymore. If I do, people will think that no one is willing to go with me."

ED abandons an activity he has enjoyed for its own sake, until now. Concern for what people might think immediately poisons a previously enjoyable activity.

EN: "I go to movies when I want to. If there is someone who can go with me, fine! Otherwise, I go by myself. After all, the point is to go to the movie, isn't it?"

EN engages in an activity he has enjoyed for its own sake. The idea that someone might think he is a loser because he is by himself never occurs to him.

Scenario 16

Future mother-in-law: I want you to know that I absolutely will not interfere in your marriage to my son.

ED future daughter-in-law: DARN RIGHT, YOU WON'T!

ED defends against an attack that never happened. Manages to upset a person who, until then, had been on her side.

EN future daughter-in-law: I really appreciate that. It was obviously an issue that occurred to me. Thank you for telling me that.

EN accepts the communication as the gift it was intended to be. In the process, she keeps an ally.

Scenario 17

Person #1: Your idea won't work.

ED: What do you mean? Of course it will! You don't know what you're talking about!

ED Victor can't admit any shortcomings. Takes constructive criticism as a personal attack. ED Victim abandons his idea. Assumes everything he does is worthless.

EN: What do you mean? I need to make this work. Would you help me out here?

EN accepts criticism as friendly, helpful input. Focuses on search for complete knowledge.

Scenario 18

ED: Nobody likes you.

EN: Some people don't like it because you do such-and-such. Maybe you don't intend it, but this behavior really upsets some people.

Describes specific behavior so it is possible to correct it. Criticism is of the behavior, rather than of the person.

Scenario 19

Person #1: Would you please keep the noise down? Some of us are trying to sleep.

ED: Go to hell!

ED reacts to this request as though it were a personal attack.

EN: Sorry! I got carried away and wasn't paying attention. Thanks for pointing it out.

EN responds to this request as though it were a request. He is grateful to be told how to make something right that he had made wrong. Then he makes it right – treating others as he wants to be treated.

Scenario 20

ED only reluctantly admits mistakes. Attempts to blame other people or circumstances when possible. Attempts to conceal mistake when there is no other place to put the blame.

EN readily admits mistakes and corrects them if possible.

Scenario 21

ED: I don't do any more than I absolutely have to do. If it's not my job, I don't do it. I'm not stupid!

EN: I've finished everything I have to do. Is there something else that needs to be done?

EN knows that the most pleasant and eager workers are typically the ones who get ahead. He realizes that by performing duties beyond his job description he is acquiring knowledge that can be transferred to other work situations. If promotion isn't forthcoming, he eventually goes somewhere with more opportunity.

Scenario 22

ED discovers a lump in her breast and phones her boyfriend about her concern, then talks to her roommate:

ED: I found a lump on my breast this morning, and I'll be seeing the doctor about it tomorrow.

Roommate: Did you tell your boyfriend yet?

ED: NO. NO. I didn't want to worry him.

ED lies in order to appear as a strong and self-sacrificing human being – bravely keeping her secret from her boyfriend so he won't worry.

EN discovers a lump in her breast and phones her boyfriend about her concern, then talks to her roommate:

EN: I found a lump on my breast this morning, and I'll be seeing the doctor about it tomorrow.

Roommate: Did you tell your boyfriend yet?

EN: Yes. I was so worried that I told him about it first thing.

EN simply relays facts. Not trying to impress anyone about anything.

Scenario 23

ED: I'm not happy about this legislation in Washington. But it's a done deal. It always is. So why waste my time contacting a congressman who won't pay attention anyway! It's stupid to waste your time on something with no payoff.

ED chooses expediency over principle.

(Note: Many of these same people ironically spend ten + dollars a week on lottery tickets!)

EN: I'm not happy about this legislation in Washington. I'm going to contact my congressman. I know one phone call won't make a big difference, but it's the one thing I can do. There's no excuse for doing less than I can do. If enough people call in, it can make a difference.

(EN acts on principle.)

Scenario 24-A

Passenger in car: Oops! I forgot to fasten my seat belt. (Reaches for seat belt.)

ED Driver: (Slams on brakes.) Well, put it on right now!

ED Passenger: (Drops belt.) I'll fasten it when I'm good and ready to fasten it.

ED Driver: We're not going *anywhere* until you fasten it!

ED Passenger: Then get ready to sit here for a very long time!

Driver's agenda is to impose control, thereby positioning himself above the passenger. Passenger's agenda is to resist control, thereby maintaining his position relative to the driver.

EN Passenger: (Fastens seatbelt since that is what he started to do. Obeying the driver has nothing to do with the belt-fastening. EN does not allow ED to control him (in reverse) by refusing to fasten his seat belt.) Out of curiosity, what did you have to gain by ordering me to do something that I had already begun to do?

EN, in a non-judgmental way, seeks full knowledge of the situation.

Scenario 24-B

Passenger in car: Oops! I forgot to fasten my seat belt. (Reaches for seat belt.)

EN Driver: (Continues driving. Says nothing.)

EN Passenger: (Fastens belt.)

Scenario 25

Passenger in car: Do you see that bike rider up ahead?

ED Driver: I'm perfectly capable of driving a car by myself! I don't need any help from you.

Driver feels that passenger has found him lacking and therefore thinks that passenger views him in a lower position. Driver responds with rage against the passenger in an attempt to maintain his pecking-order position.

EN Passenger: Gee! When someone tries to help me, I usually say, "Thank you."

Passenger is unconcerned with his pecking-order position when ED Driver reacts with anger.

EN Driver: Thanks for mentioning it. I did see him, but I'd prefer that you point out something I might not see, rather than just sit in silence and maybe let something ugly happen.

EN Driver is not concerned with defending his self-image. He perceives the warning about the bike rider as information instead of judgment.

Scenario 26

ED: I want to get certified for this specialty, but I'm afraid to take the test because I might fail. So, I'm not even going to try.

EN: I really want to get certified for this specialty, but I might not pass the test. Well, I'll just keep on taking the test until I pass! I'm not going to let a setback keep me from eventually getting where I really want to be.

Scenario 27

ED: I'm so mad at Joe I'm never going to speak to him again! I don't care how many times he asks me what he did to make me mad. That'll fix him. Besides, it's more fun to be mad than to resolve the issue.

EN: I'm so mad at Joe I don't want to ever speak to him again! But I've got to get past that and tell him why I'm angry. If we don't communicate, this upset will fester forever.

EN keeps lines of communication opened. Seeks full knowledge of the situation.

Scenario 28

Someone lights a cigarette in a non-smoking area.

ED: You can't smoke here! What do you think you're doing?!!! Who do you think you are?!!!

EN Smoker: Sorry. I didn't notice. (extinguishes cigarette)

EN: Excuse me, but this is a non-smoking section.

ED Smoker: I'll smoke anywhere I *bleep* please! No one tells me what to do! No one tells me where I can and can't smoke!

EN: Excuse me, but this is a non-smoking section.

EN Smoker: Sorry. I didn't notice. (extinguishes cigarette)

Scenario 29: Self-esteem

ED: I want to feel better about myself.

EN: I want to feel better.

Feelings about himself are not an active issue. In this way, negative feelings about himself cannot corrupt the experience of feeling good and excessive excitement arising from ego-aggrandizement cannot distort the experience of feeling good.

Scenario 30

A solution to a problem has just been presented at a business meeting. Another participant states, "There is another possible way to address this problem."

ED: I don't give a damn what you think. We're doing it my way!

EN: What is it? Let's discuss both ideas.